AF283973

ENGLAND
The Mini-Book of Aerial Views

First published 2005

Reprinted 2006, 2007

LAST REFUGE Ltd.

© Adrian Warren and Dae Sasitorn, 2005

This book was designed and produced by

Last Refuge Ltd.

Batch Farm, Panborough, near Wells, Somerset, BA5 1PN, UK, tel: (44) (0) 1934 712556

e-mail: info@lastrefuge.co.uk, www.lastrefuge.co.uk

Designers:

Dae Sasitorn

Will Brett

Front cover: *Alton Barnes White Horse, Wiltshire*

Back cover: *Stonehenge, Uffington White Horse, Badbury Rings, Housesteads Roman Fort,*
Fountains Abbey, Lulworth Cove, The Wash, Rainbow over Somerset Levels, The Needles, Wast Water,
St Michael's Mount, Arundel Castle, M25/M23 Junction, Centre Court Wimbledon, Otterburn

All photographs in this book are available for publication or as prints from www.lastrefuge.co.uk

ISBN: 0-9544350-5-2

Printed and bound by Compass Press, China

ENGLAND
The Mini-Book of Aerial Views

ADRIAN WARREN & DAE SASITORN

LAST REFUGE

For Oliver, Sean and Luke

CONTENTS

PREFACE

This is a miniature edition of our big book: *ENGLAND – An Aerial View*, which we published last year. The text is shorter and the captions are simple but this mini-book is much lighter to carry! When we began working on the big book, I suddenly realised how little I knew about my own country. For Dae, England is not her native land, so she had an excuse, but the same did not apply to me. During the three hundred hours of flying it took to do the photography, our eyes were opened as each new horizon unfolded. It was a journey of discovery to see the changing landscapes, places, and the history that was laid out before us. The historic sites particularly grabbed our attention. Over the course of millennia, the English landscape has been altered dramatically by the passage of time and the successive waves of people who have made it their home. Although the face of England today bears little resemblance to how it looked when early settlers arrived, the signs of their passing are still visible. This book is a time slice – a portrait of modern England sitting alongside the evidence of hundreds, even thousands, of years of history.

The photographs in this book were taken with a Hasselblad 6 x 6 cm medium format camera using Fuji Velvia transparency film. The camera was handheld in the large open window of our aircraft (except over London where we were obliged to use a helicopter) using a special rig we built with two handles to help keep the camera steady. Aerial photography is demanding. It is a strange environment for a photographer and one where it is necessary to be calm, relaxed and confident whatever manoeuvre the aircraft is making. While Dae undertook the photography, I concentrated on the flying. Photographer and pilot, two people working as a team, each one understanding the needs of the other. For Dae, the challenge is about light and composition, for me it is to try to put her in a good position for the shot.

Safety is the most important consideration however. Aerial photography often requires working the aircraft close to its aerodynamic limits. Every pilot knows that an engine failure can happen at any moment so, with a single engine aircraft like our Cessna 182, one must always be prepared for emergency procedures throughout any flight. Over mountains, or over the sea, I tend to listen to the hum of the engine very carefully. We bought the aircraft in 1999 and our Cessna has become a trusty friend. Many of our photographic flights last in excess of five hours in order to make the most of good weather conditions. In the winter it can be freezing cold flying with the window open, but in the summer, especially on a warm summers evening with the red sun sinking on the horizon, it is a wonderful experience to be in the sky, steering homewards in the direction of our little farm strip in Somerset following a satisfying shoot.

Adrian Warren & Dae Sasitorn
Somerset, England
August 2005

Lulworth Cove, Dorset

1: THE ESSENCE OF ENGLAND

".... England's green and pleasant land." (William Blake, 1757-1827)

We are flying in our small aeroplane, somewhere over rural England. As far as the eye can see, a gently rolling patchwork of fields, interspersed with pockets of woodland, stretches into the distance. Everything, it seems, is a pleasant shade of green. As seen from the ground, before we took off, the landscape was only visible from a narrow perspective, but as the aircraft climbed, the countryside unfolded like a map. When flying over England, it is surprising that there is so much open space on a small island providing a home for some fifty million people. More amazing, however, is how secrets of the past are revealed when viewed from above. Traces of human activity going back thousands of years, where long forgotten hands and ancient ploughs once worked the land, can still be seen from the air as lines of earthworks, contours, or ghostly marks in the soil and many archaeological sites have only been discovered by chance observation from an aircraft. England has a complex and fascinating history. To see actual traces of events that happened a long time ago brings them to life, but our green and pleasant land is now disappearing beneath the hungry spread of cities, towns and industrial areas linked by ever growing networks of roads. The face of England is changing more rapidly now than ever before in human history. The growth in population is revealing. In 1066, at the time of the Norman invasion by William the Conqueror, there were about 1 million people in England. Over the next 700 years, to 1800, the population grew to 9 million but only 200 years later, in 2001, the census showed 49 million, equivalent to 379 people per square kilometre (984 per square mile).

The first Stone Age hunters ventured across the dry English Channel from the Continent at least 650,000 years ago. Those early settlers found refuge in caves, emerging to hunt mammoth, rhinoceros, and hippopotamus. Lions and hyenas would have been formidable enemies. From 480,000 years ago, England was gripped by frequent dramatic changes in the climate from subtropical to arctic as ice sheets repeatedly advanced and retreated. The temperature changes caused the sea level to fluctuate, which would have led to the sporadic isolation of Britain from the rest of Europe. This would explain the apparent absence of people from Britain for quite long periods when the land bridge was broken. In fact, for a period of 100,000 years, there is no evidence of human presence at all. It seems that the advancing ice sheet 150,000 years ago pushed people out and, later, the rising sea level delayed their return. The transitions were sometimes extremely rapid, perhaps even comparable to a human lifespan, a phenomenon of which we should take careful note given our present climatic trends. Climate change can have a catastrophic effect, not only on human populations but also on animal and plant life.

It was not until about 13,000 years ago that modern humans established a permanent footing here. As the last of the ice slowly retreated, the temperature rose, trees grew, and by 7000 BC, much of England was covered by verdant, deciduous forest. Melting ice caused the sea level to rise, and Britain became an island, cut off from the Continent of Europe by the North Sea and the English Channel. Around 4000 BC, the first farmers arrived from the Continent. These people mined flint for making tools, traded goods between their communities, and cleared large areas of forest, cultivating the soil with simple wooden ploughs. By 1000 BC considerable tree clearance had taken place for growing crops like wheat and barley, and pasture for cattle and sheep. Then, a steady flow of new immigrants arrived, introducing the use of copper and bronze to make tools and weapons. They created irregular, rounded fields, clearing the land of stones, which they occasionally used to build foundations for houses, and for dry stone walls to protect their settlements. They also created many mysterious circles of wood or stone of ritual significance, among them, in Wiltshire, the great henge at Avebury, and Stonehenge, arguably the finest Bronze Age temple in Europe.

Celtic people began to arrive around 600 BC, bringing with them the skill to work with iron and introducing iron ploughs to farming in Britain. Iron Age fields of that period, some of which still exist today, were long and narrow to reduce the number of times it was necessary to turn oxen and plough around. Farming was becoming quite efficient and sophisticated, with an increasing variety of crops and domesticated animals. The Celts, though, were warriors, as intent on raiding and plundering each other as attacking other tribes. In order to deter invaders, communities were frequently sited in hilltop forts, protected by a system of deep ditches and high banks topped by wooden stakes. Many of these hill forts have stood the test of time and their outlines remain etched on the landscape even today. Some grew to massive proportions with complex and impressive defences such as those at Maiden Castle in Dorset. The Celts also carved giant hill figures. Normally associated with hill forts, these figures were typically created on chalk downs by scraping away the topsoil to reveal the white chalk underneath, and the resulting images were visible over great distances. The simple, though artistic, bold lines of the white horse at Uffington, in Oxfordshire, have adorned the landscape since before 100 BC.

Julius Caesar made a brief exploratory mission to Britain in 55 BC and a little under 100 years later, the Romans invaded with a powerful force. They made their mark on the landscape quickly, crushing resistance in much of England. As they advanced, they built forts, towns, and paved roads for communication. They also mined the land for valuable resources such as lead and tin, much of which was exported to the Roman Empire on the Continent. By AD 80, they had reached Scotland, and in order to protect their northern frontier against attack they built the famous Hadrian's Wall over about four years, starting in AD 122. The Roman occupation was withdrawn in AD 407, but in less than 400 years, the landscape of England had become indelibly changed. As soon as the Romans left, the native peoples were in a state of chaos. In the absence of Roman defences, the country was attacked from all sides: by Scots from Ireland, Picts from Scotland, as well as Angle and Saxon tribes from the Continent. Vikings, too – pagan Norwegian, Swedish and Danish warriors, raided and began to settle in eastern parts of England by the late eighth century. This was a period of conflict, pillage, massacre and confusion when, bombarded by different racial influences from all sides, our linguistic and cultural diversity was established. Finally, a Germanic people became dominant. To the Celts, all Germanic people were referred to as Saxons, although in the end Britain came to be called 'England' after the Angles. By AD 600, Anglo-Saxon invaders had settled most of England with the exception of the far west, and were busy building the villages that would form the basic plan of our modern day landscape.

When William the Conqueror invaded in 1066, England was not only old but wealthy, an attractive acquisition in this time of opportunist expansion. William's violent conquest was designed to subdue any resistance. For years following the Battle of Hastings, the country lived in fear, for his forces traveled everywhere plundering and killing indiscriminately. It was William's greed that led to the Domesday Book project, which set out to record the value of every parcel of land in England, forming a unique portrait of English social history at that time. The Normans were great castle and church builders, and they brought new technical skills in the design of arches and vaults. It was in the thirteenth century that church steeples made their first appearance in English villages. There is no doubt that church building aroused community spirit through the enthusiasm, creative abilities and sense of pride among the people. In towns where castles were built, populations grew to supply craftsmen to build and furnish them, as well as to manufacture weapons.

In 1347, bubonic and pneumonic plague reached the Mediterranean after a Kipchak army, besieging a Genoese trading post in the Crimea, catapulted plague infested corpses into the town. From Mediterranean ports, the disease spread quickly northwards. It became known as the Black Death, and as it ravaged through Europe it killed an estimated 25 million people, about a third of the entire population, in just five years. In Britain, well over a million people died, causing massive social problems and the total annihilation of at least 1,000 villages in England, the traces of which can still be seen from the air. The plague period of 1347–1352 was probably the worst natural disaster ever recorded in human history.

The Industrial Revolution of the eighteenth and nineteenth centuries brought dramatic change as new mines and quarries were dug to exploit natural resources. The extraction of coal produced mountainous, black spoil heaps; and quarrying of white china clay in Cornwall formed a moonscape known locally as the Cornish Alps. The need to transport the natural resources to the factories resulted in the building of canals and railway networks, leaving more indelible marks on the landscape in the shape of locks, embankments, cuttings, bridges, and stations. Between 1750 and 1850, the Enclosure Acts re-shaped rural England, introducing a change in farming methods to increase productivity in order to feed expanding urban populations. The new fields, about 4 hectares (10 acres) in size, were enclosed by stone walls or hedges to give the landscape the familiar look that it has today. The creation of hedgerows also encouraged wildlife by providing sites for birds to nest, and natural, safe corridors for small terrestrial animals.

England was at one time almost completely covered by dense forests of oak, ash, lime, alder, elm and hazel, so many of our plants and animals are woodland species. Ever since neolithic times, people have tamed the land by felling trees. During the Middle Ages, as demand for timber increased, great swathes of forest were felled and the land turned over to agricultural use. Woodland may have diminished but is still a significant feature of the English landscape, although it only covers a tiny fraction of the area it once did, and much of today's forests are monocultures of introduced softwoods, no substitute for the natural woodland, so essential for the conservation of our indigenous wildlife.

The twentieth century saw a growing population with an ever-increasing standard of living, resulting in massive housing projects, together with an infrastructure of electric pylons and telegraph wires, huge reservoirs, and power stations. The development of the internal combustion engine triggered the building of complex networks of roads and airports. The invention of plastic added to the growing problem of processing waste and landfill sites became familiar eyesores in the landscape. Today, England is already in a new post-industrial transition in which mass concentrations of people in urban workplaces are in decline due to automation and computers. However, away from the cities and motorways, in peaceful corners of rural England, there is a mature landscape in which our history is still laid out vividly. Whether it is a church or castle, cottage or manor, stone wall or ruin, path or field, it has probably been there for centuries. Stone and wood, mellowed by moss and lichen, and cracked by the passing of many winters and summers, blend comfortably into their surroundings. Each has its own story to tell. Much of English history is beautifully, if subtly, preserved and awaits discovery by anyone who takes the time to look.

Cerne Abbas Giant, Dorset

II: THE SOUTH COUNTRY

Berkshire, Dorset, Hampshire, the Isle of Wight, Wiltshire

The South Country has retained spectacular visual evidence of its ancient history, but it is losing that connection faster than any other region of England. In the face of modern development, fast roads and, in the eastern parts, the proximity of London, it is playing host to ever increasing numbers of people who only use it as a place to sleep. The countryside here is liberally sprinkled with obvious signs of early human presence in burial mounds, hill forts and monuments. The smooth, open, grassy contours of the South Downs and the Marlborough Downs, and the sweeping grassland of Salisbury Plain hide little from view. This part of England was intensively colonised, for many people arriving from the continent of Europe must have passed through or settled in this region. Here are many of the classic sites of archaeology: Stonehenge, Avebury, Maiden Castle, and the Badbury Rings.

From earliest times, people have created works of art as paintings on cave walls and as carvings on rocks. It was, perhaps, a natural progression to draw huge figures in the landscape. England has more hill figures than any other country in the world, including two giants and some fourteen white horses, most of which occur in the south of England. One wonders how many more of these works of art have been lost through the passage of time. The South Country is an ideal place for them since there is so much chalk downland; the topsoil here is quite shallow, and by scraping it away to expose the white chalk underneath it is possible to create a dazzling mark that can be seen from a great distance. The hill figures are mysterious, their purpose uncertain. Many are associated with hill fort settlements and may have been totems or talismans for the communities. They may also have acted as landmarks for travelers, positioned as they were on steep hillsides so they could be seen from afar. But the figures needed frequent maintenance to prevent their gradual disappearance through erosion and becoming overgrown with weeds. During this process, they would have tended to change their shape, and because of the regular disturbance to the soil they are difficult to age with any certainty. No one knows who carved the famous Cerne Abbas Giant in Dorset; it was not formally documented until 1694 when a local churchwarden referred to the cost of its maintenance, although it could date back to the Iron Age. Its naked figure was characteristic of Celtic warriors, who often went into battle without clothes and with their bodies daubed with blue dye. The giant's prominent phallus suggests it may also have been a fertility symbol, and many myths and legends surround this fascinating hill figure.

During the Iron Age of the Celts, horses symbolized power, beauty, and prosperity. Horse designs even appear on Iron Age coins. The white horse hill figure at Westbury, in Wiltshire, as we see it today, was created in 1778 and is superimposed on a much older figure, which, it seems, faced the opposite direction. The original figure was associated with the adjacent Iron Age hill fort of Bratton Camp and also the legendary site of the Battle of Ethandune in AD 848, when King Alfred defeated the Danes. As at Westbury, most of the visible hill figures today are not ancient – they have been created, or re-created, since around 1750.

Another kind of giant figure has, in recent years, adorned our landscape during the summer months. Crop circles, where crops have been neatly flattened to create an interesting shape, have suddenly appeared overnight in the middle of large fields of maturing cereal crops with no apparent clue as to how they were formed. It has been suggested that they are the marks left by alien spacecraft, but, in reality, crop circles are works of art created anonymously, by small teams of skilled artists, under the cover of darkness. The craft of circle making requires detailed planning, the use of accurate surveying techniques and simple flattening tools. They can appear anywhere and are intended to function as temporary sacred sites, and sometimes a bit of fun, but the nucleus of activity is the area of Avebury, in Wiltshire, which has held religious and mystical significance for millennia. The great henge enclosure at Avebury, on the Marlborough Downs, represents an important sacred site for ritual and worship dating back to around 2000 BC. Nearby is the enigmatic Silbury Hill, which at 40 metres (130 feet) high is the largest prehistoric man-made mound in Britain, dating back to at least 2700 BC. Close to Silbury Hill, and about the same age, is West Kennet Long Barrow, a neolithic burial place where massive blocks of rock guard the largest chambered tomb in England. Through aerial photography, over the years, more circles, monuments and enclosures have been discovered, and much more investigative work still needs to be done in this fascinating area.

To the south of the Marlborough Downs is the broad Vale of Pewsey, its flanks decorated by several white horse figures. Further south still are the high sweeping grasslands of Salisbury Plain. Here are yet more historic sites: among them the greatest megalithic monument in Europe, Stonehenge. Now a World Heritage Site, it is unique, unlike anything anywhere else in the world. The huge stones stand stark and silent, as they have done for thousands of years. Many have pondered as to its purpose but it seems certain that Stonehenge was a sophisticated temple, already ancient by the time the Romans arrived in England. It was built in three phases, the first beginning around 3000 BC, when a circular ditch and bank were created. This was followed, a few hundred years later, by phase two, when a wooden structure was erected. Phase three began around 2500 BC, when blue stones were brought all the way from the Prescelly Mountains in South Wales, an incredible feat at that time. Large Sarsen stones were also hauled to the site on the Marlborough Downs to the north and erected as trilithons (two vertical blocks of rock supporting a third one laid horizontally) in a circle with a continuous lintel. Five more trilithons were erected in the centre in the shape of a horseshoe and the structure was completed around 1500 BC. The people who planned Stonehenge so long ago were far more sophisticated than we might imagine. Without the aid of telescopes, compasses, sextants or computers, they measured the movements of the sun and moon, the changing length of days and nights through the seasons, and positioned the stones with great accuracy to mark significant risings or settings of the sun and moon. As a result, Stonehenge gave them the ability to anticipate the arrival of winter and summer, and even to forecast eclipses of the moon. For centuries, it must have been an overwhelmingly powerful and important place for farming communities whose lives were governed by the seasons.

Adjacent to Stonehenge, a large area of Salisbury Plain has been annexed as a military training area. Ironically, this is good news for both the landscape and the wildlife, for it has allowed the natural habitat to remain relatively undisturbed save for a few tank tracks and bomb craters. So, instead of farmland with monocultures of wheat, barley or rape, the area is the realm of skylark, nightingale, wheatear and stone curlew. Now, the great bustard, the heaviest flying bird in the world, which disappeared from the British countryside in the 1870s, has been re-introduced and will hopefully once more wander freely across the open Plain. Prized as a game bird, great bustards were once widely distributed in England, but hunting and the intensification of agriculture in the nineteenth century led to its extinction.

The Isle of Wight is England's smallest county, displaying a certain old world charm. It is an English landscape in miniature, surrounded by sandy bays, high cliffs and sheltered inlets. The Romans favoured it for its mild climate and strategically important position, constructing large villas and growing vineyards. In the seventeenth century, King Charles I was imprisoned at Carisbrooke Castle at the heart of the island prior to his execution by Oliver Cromwell. Queen Victoria's country palace at Osborne was one of her favourite places, and her presence brought prosperity to the island in the nineteenth century. Today, the main source of income is the seasonal hotel trade for tourists.

Since the Second World War, Hampshire has changed dramatically. Towns and villages here expanded to accommodate the burgeoning work force of London, its commuters travelling back and forth along the networks of roads and rail networks. In the west of Hampshire is the New Forest, one of the oldest and largest Royal hunting forests, with oak, birch, beech and stretches of heathland. The coastline of Hampshire includes the deep-water estuaries of the Hamble and Beaulieu rivers, popular with yachting enthusiasts. Portsmouth became an important harbour for the Royal Navy in the seventeenth century and from there, many British fleets have set sail to go to war. In the nineteenth century, Southampton became the most important passenger shipping port in Britain. Winchester was an important town in Roman times; under the Anglo-Saxons, it became capital of Wessex, and under William the Conqueror, the capital of England. Winchester has managed to preserve much of its antiquity, a medieval city with a cathedral where twelve English kings are buried. Many Hampshire villages have preserved the classic grouping of a village green around which are the church, vicarage, school and manor house. Some still have wide main streets, broad enough to turn a coach drawn by a team of horses.

Berkshire has seen perhaps the greatest changes in its landscape, mainly due to its proximity to London. 3,000 years ago, from their trading route along the crest of the Berkshire Downs, ancient Britons looked down on a sea of forest and scrub, which would gradually be transformed into today's tamed landscape of villages and market towns. By the fourteenth century, the relative importance of towns was reflected in the facilities they possessed for handling river traffic, which was at that time an important lifeline for trade. Medieval Berkshire also became well supplied with roads. In 1360, when the oldest known official map of Britain was drawn, the road to Bath and Bristol carried trading caravans, laden with supplies of cloth, to the big markets in Bristol and London.

Of the southern counties, Dorset is furthest from London and is not over-run by major roads or motorways. This land of Thomas Hardy is a rich patchwork of fields and hills with quaint villages and thatched cottages. High chalk downland with rounded slopes punctuate the lush, fertile pastures. On hill tops and ridges are some of the most magnificent ancient hill forts, for example Maiden Castle near Dorchester, with its complex and multi-layered system of protective ramparts. To the east of Dorchester is acid heathland, which once stretched almost unbroken from here, through Hampshire as far as Surrey, an important habitat for Britain's rare lizards and snakes. On the Dorset coast, where the chalk downs meet the sea, is a dramatic coastline where pounding seas have carved and sculpted the cliffs into interesting shapes, as at Durdle Door and, a little further east, the magnificent natural harbour at Lulworth Cove. To the west of Portland is Chesil beach – a great, scimitar-shaped barrier of shingle. The coast of Dorset westwards to Devon is world famous as the Jurassic Coast, a World Heritage Site providing an almost continuous geological record of earth history from 251 to 66 million years ago.

New Devizes White Horse, Wiltshire

Oldbury White Horse and Camp, Wiltshire

Westbury Quarry and Westbury White Horse in the background, Wiltshire

Westbury White Horse and Bratton Camp, Wiltshire

Osmington White Horse, Dorset

Alton Barnes White Horse, Wiltshire

N 51° 19' 31" W 001° 45' 01"   Map Ref: 4 14   Grid Ref: SU175585

New Pewsey White Horse, Wiltshire

Winterbourne Bassett White Horse, Wiltshire

N 51° 24' 55" W 001° 44' 07"   Map Ref: 4 13   Grid Ref: SU185685

Marlborough (Preshute) White Horse, Wiltshire

Oldbury White Horse, Wiltshire

Badbury Rings, Dorset

Bury Hill, Hampshire

N 51° 11' 07" W 001° 29' 19" Map Ref. A K5 Grid Ref. SU346436

Danebury Ring, Hampshire

Beacon Hill Fort, Hampshire

Ladle Hill Fort, Hampshire

Eggardon Hill Fort, Dorset

Maiden Castle, Dorset

Scratchbury Hill Fort, Wiltshire

Battlesbury Camp Hill Fort, Wiltshire

Yarnbury Castle, Wiltshire

N 50° 53' 45" W 001° 57' 44"   Map Ref: 4 H8   Grid Ref: SU027107

Knowlton Circles, Dorset

Old Sarum, Wiltshire

N 51° 05' 20" W 001° 48' 23"   Map Ref: 4 16   Grid Ref: SU136321

Silbury Hill, Wiltshire

Stonehenge, Wiltshire

Poor Lot Barrows, Dorset

N 50° 42′ 32″ W 002°

N 51° 25′ 44″ W 001° 50′ 56″   Map Ref: 4 12   Grid Ref: SU106700

Avebury, Wiltshire

West Kennet Long Barrow, Wiltshire

N 51° 24' 30"   W 001° 50' 54"   Map Ref: 4 H3   Grid Ref: SU106677

N 51° 10' 13"   W 001°

Normanton Down Barrows, Wiltshire

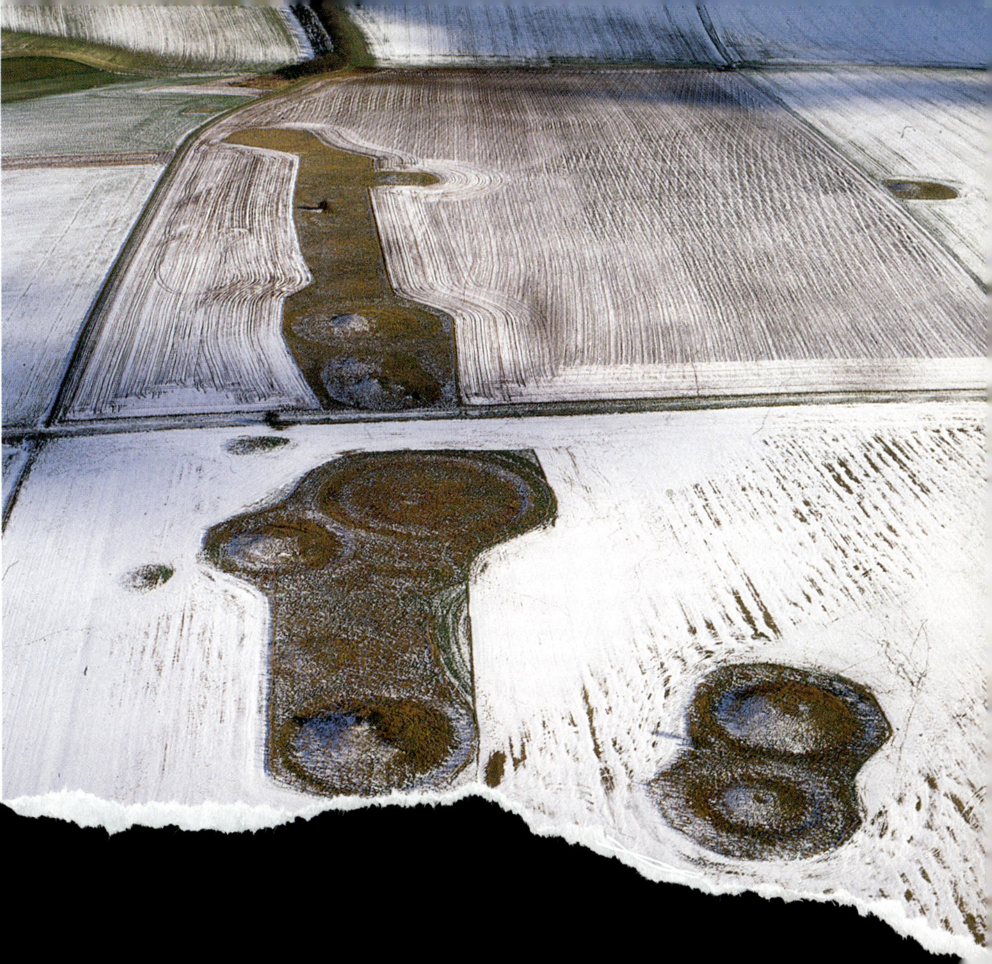

9' 45"   Map Ref: 4 I6   Grid Ref: SU120412

N 51° 24' 31" W 001° 56' 04"   Map Ref: 4 H3   Grid Ref: SU047677

Barrows at North Down, near Calstone Wellington, Wiltshire

43

Wansdyke, Tan Hill, Wiltshire

N 51° 22' 46" W 001° 51' 54"   Map Ref: 4 H3   Grid Ref: SU095643

Crop Circle, Wiltshire

Crop Circle, Wiltshire

Crop Circle, Wiltshire

Crop Circle, Wiltshire

Crop Circles, Wiltshire

Artwork in a wheatfield at Yatesbury, Wiltshire

N 51° 22' 13" W 001° 46' 43"   Map Ref: 4 13   Grid Ref: SU155635

Heart Orchard, Huish Hill, near Oare, Wiltshire

Pig Farm, Wiltshire

Harvest, Wiltshire

Portsmouth, Hampshire

N 50° 47' 29" W 001° 04' 19"   Map Ref: 5 C10   Grid Ref: SZ657992

HM Naval Base, Portsmouth, Hampshire

Bucklers Hard, Hampshire

N 50° 47′ 52″ W 001° 25′ 27″   Map Ref: 4 L10   Grid Ref: SZ406999

Salisbury, Wiltshire

Longford Castle, Wiltshire

N 51° 02' 15" W 001° 45' 06"   Map Ref: 417   Grid Ref: SU175265

N 51° 02' 13" W 002° 05' 07"   Map Ref: 4 G7   Grid Ref: ST941264

Old Wardour Castle, Wiltshire

Sherborne Old Castle, Dorset

N 50° 56' 53" W 002° 29' 50"   Map Ref: 4 D8   Grid Ref: ST651166

Sherborne New Castle, Dorset

Corfe Castle, Dorset

N 50° 38' 28"   W 002° 04' 00"   Map Ref: 4 G11   Grid Ref: SY953823

Basing House, Hampshire

Breamore House, Hampshire

N 50° 58′ 21″ W 001° 47′ 03″   Map Ref: 4 18   Grid Ref: SU152192

Rockbourne Roman Villa, Hampshire

Osborne House, Isle of Wight

N 50° 45' 01" W 001° 15' 58"   Map Ref: 5 B11   Grid Ref: SZ518947

Carisbrooke Castle, Isle of Wight

The Needles, Isle of Wight

N 50° 39' 47" W 001° 35' 39" Map Ref: 4 J11 Grid Ref: SZ287848

Lulworth Cove, Dorset

Durdle Door, Dorset

N 50° 37' 26"   W 002° 16' 37"   Map Ref: 4 F11   Grid Ref: SY805805

Portland Bill, Dorset

Old Harry Rocks, Dorset

N 50° 38' 32" W 001° 55' 25"   Map Ref: 4 H11   Grid Ref: SZ055825

N 50° 37' 55" W 002° 33' 35"   Map Ref: 4 D11   Grid Ref: SY605815

Chesil Beach, Dorset

Glastonbury Tor, Somerset

N 51° 08' 37" W 002° 41' 41"   Map Ref: 4 C6   Grid Ref: ST515385

III: THE WEST COUNTRY

Cornwall, Devon, Somerset

The South West of England is steeped in history and in legend. It is said that Joseph of Arimathea visited Glastonbury, in Somerset, in AD 31 and built the first Christian church in England there. He brought the Holy Grail with him, burying it at the foot of Glastonbury Tor where a spring has flowed ever since with water that is tinted red by Christ's blood. He also planted his staff, which sprouted to become the celebrated Holy Thorn that grows on a grassy ridge just south of the town. Whether Joseph came or not, Glastonbury became recognised as a Christian monastic site by Romans and Saxons alike, and has held mystic and religious significance ever since. Among the many other legends of the South West, the story of King Arthur has been embedded in mystery for centuries. There is no proof of his existence, but he is reputed to have been born at Tintagel, in Cornwall, led the people against invading Saxons and, following his death at the battle of Camlan in AD 539, was buried at Glastonbury.

The north and south coastlines of the south west peninsula could not be more different; to the north, the River Severn empties its muddy brown waters into the Bristol Channel with a spectacular tidal rise and fall, reputed to be the second highest in the world. To the south is the English Channel, widening in the west to meet the Atlantic and bordered by beaches, cliffs, and rocky coves. The climate benefits from the warm Atlantic Gulf Stream, which brings mild, though rather wet, weather all year round and rainfall at least double that of southeast England. The prevailing winds, warmed by a long passage over the Atlantic, bring rain clouds, form sea mists along the coast and hill fogs on the moors. Gales from Biscay and the Atlantic drive furiously across the narrow peninsula in Cornwall, so trees are tortured and stunted, while the ground is covered by plants like heather and grass that can survive the punishment. At first glance, much of the landscape seems bleak and untamed, but there are many deep valleys, often steep-sided and in parts well wooded, providing shelter for a wealth of plants. The rarity of winter frosts permits the growth of exotic subtropical plants in private gardens. The principal rivers flow southwards, to a coastline indented by a succession of deep estuaries and natural harbours, which are, in fact, flooded valleys caused by the rise in sea level following the retreat of Ice Age glaciers.

Cornwall is rich in minerals, more so than anywhere else in Britain with tin, copper, iron, lead, gold, silver and many others including uranium. For centuries, tin mining was one of the mainstays of Cornwall's economy. However, since the seams of ore ran steeply downwards in the granite to well below the surface of the sea, water seeped into the mineshafts and had to be removed by powerful pumps. The now derelict tall chimneys and engine houses are reminders of a once thriving though perilous industry. Gold grains in streams, together with tin, lead, and copper, drew the attentions of Bronze Age voyagers and settlers to this part of England after 2500 BC. The many natural harbours made the South West attractive to those arriving by boat from the Continent. Ancient Greek coins discovered in Devon suggest frequent trade with merchants from as far away as the Mediterranean. A considerable degree of local culture would have been derived from contact with these traders; indeed, the Bronze Age peoples of Devon and Cornwall may have seen more foreigners than visitors from elsewhere in England.

Somerset is rich in pasture: Saxon farmers brought their cattle to graze here over 1,300 years ago. Bounded on the north by the Mendip Hills, with their spectacular caves and gorges, is the peat-rich marshland of the Somerset Levels, the legendary Isle of Avalon, and Glastonbury. To the south west are the sandstone masses of the Quantock Hills, which are famed for their red deer, the Blackdown Hills, the Brendon Hills and beautiful Exmoor, which extends into Devon. There, the north coast is dramatic with high cliffs rising abruptly from the Atlantic surf while the south coast is luxuriant and colourful, with a patchwork of fields reaching down to the sea in between the many resort towns and villages. Inland, Devon is a network of narrow lanes, winding, climbing and descending hills and valleys, and dominated by the huge, brooding granite mass of Dartmoor with several high points above 600 metres (about 2,000 feet). There are four more granite moorlands in Cornwall: Bodmin Moor, the St. Austell Highlands (famous for china clay), Carnmenellis, and St Just near Land's End. The Scilly Isles could be called yet another granite moor of which only the highest points remain above the sea.

The beautiful Scillies form a charming and exotic archipelago of over 150 islands and islets that lie 40 kilometres (25 miles) off the tip of Cornwall. Famed for their mild climate, white sandy beaches and turquoise clear waters, it is a curious fact that more people lived on the islands in ancient times than today. The place is littered with Bronze Age barrows and hut circles, some of them submerged in the shallow waters, indicating that the sea level has risen over the last four millennia, and indeed is continuing to rise. The islands are also littered with shipwrecks. For centuries, smuggling was the main source of income for the islanders, but today the economy relies largely on tourism and the export of flowers. In contrast to the Scillies, Lundy Island, off the north coast of Devon, is rugged and remote, with the ambience of a true oceanic island.

Around 600,000 years ago, the caves of the Mendip Hills, in Somerset, offered safe refuge for early human settlers. Although the same size as modern humans, their skulls were different from ours, with thick-bones and a massive brow ridge. *Homo heidelbergensis* had emerged from Africa to reach southern Europe by about 800,000 years ago and gradually spread northwards. The hunters killed reindeer, mammoth and woolly rhinoceros using spears, and butchered the meat with simple flint tools. Successive waves of hunter gatherers came and went, driven south as the ice sheets advanced and moving north again as they receded. Neanderthals, *Homo neanderthalensis*, also lived here, but became extinct around 30,000 years ago. By about 13,000 years ago, following the retreating ice of the last Ice Age, people were here to stay. Britain's oldest known complete skeleton was buried in Gough's Cave in the Cheddar Gorge 9,000 years ago, and was only discovered in 1903. Tests conducted in 1997, which compared the DNA from 'Cheddar Man' to that of local people living in Cheddar today, actually established a match with DNA from schoolteacher Adrian Targett, suggesting that Cheddar Man still has direct descendants living in the area.

By 6000 BC, the ice had melted sufficiently to raise the sea level, separating Britain from Europe, and the Somerset Levels became inundated by seawater from the Bristol Channel. Small hilltops in the area became islands, providing refuges for hunters and gatherers who used dugouts or rafts to cross the flooded areas, which later became marshes. Around 4000 BC, farming communities became established in Britain, and reached Somerset. They constructed elevated trackways, fashioned from timber, across the marshes, to enable movement on foot between settlements and hunting areas. The oldest known is the Sweet Track, named after Ray Sweet, a peat farmer, who discovered it in 1970. Dating methods using tree rings and climate data have concluded it was built around 3806 BC and is the oldest known road in the world. The character of the Somerset Levels is one of periodic flooding, today not by the sea but during the winter rains when river and drainage systems become overwhelmed. The thick layers of peat have been cut for at least 1,000 years to be used for animal bedding or dried in blocks for fuel. At the beginning of the twentieth century, demand grew for its use in horticulture and following the Second World War output increased dramatically as mechanised diggers were used. The machines cut trenches then the peat was stacked neatly to one side in blocks to dry. From the air, the geometrical patterns formed by the dark peat and gleaming water in the flooded trenches remain a lasting symbol of the Levels around the River Brue.

The South West is rich in stone circles, hill forts, burial mounds, and ancient settlements, which are all clearly seen from the air. At Stanton Drew, just to the south of Bristol, are stone circles and avenues dating back to 2200 BC representing a centre for worship comparable to that at Avebury in Wiltshire. On the Mendip Hills are the Priddy circles and barrows, another religious site dating back to around 2000 BC. One of the best-preserved Bronze Age settlement sites is at Grimspound on Dartmoor, which dates from around 1000 BC. Within a roughly circular, stone walled area of about 1.5 hectares (4 acres), are the remains of twenty-four houses, each with low stone walls which would have supported roofs made from timber and thatched with heather and turf.

When the Iron Age Celts arrived, they fortified hill after hill with massive earthworks to protect their communities from raids, while at the same time subjugating the existing inhabitants in the area. Even when the Romans came, the Celts stood their ground to maintain what must have been an uneasy and volatile peace. As a result, Roman influence in Devon and Cornwall was light. They kept a garrison at Exeter, built minor roads to penetrate further west, and a few troops were billeted at signal stations on the north Devon coast near Countisbury and Martinhoe. In Somerset, however, the Romans began mining and smelting lead in the Mendips within a few years of arriving in England. It had already been mined here on a smaller scale for some time, as is evident by more than thirty lead objects found during the excavation of the Iron Age Lake Village on the Somerset Levels at Glastonbury. Glastonbury and Meare lake villages, built at some distance from dry land and only accessible by boat, were established by 400 BC. Dwellings were built on mounds of clay to keep them dry. Around AD 250, during the Roman occupation of Britain, an inundation from the Bristol Channel brought sea water and clay silt onto the Levels forcing the people to move elsewhere. One of the finest excavated Iron Age villages in the South West is at Chysauster in Cornwall. Dating back to 200 BC, it was still inhabited during the Roman occupation. The layout of the village can be seen very clearly. It consists of four pairs of circular courtyard houses with walls built from stone, showing considerable sophistication in design. The occupants probably mined tin from nearby streams to sell to foreign merchants at the busy port at St Michael's Mount.

The Celtic language persisted in Cornwall until the eighteenth century. Although the Celts had held out against the Romans and the Saxons, they were finally 'subdued' by the Normans. The resilient Cornish, however, continued to rebel against all those they considered outsiders from 'up-country' England, so Cornwall became a lawless backwater. Apart from mining and fishing, smuggling was one of the main activities until the nineteenth century. Before the railway improved overland communication, travellers would often make the journey to Cornwall from Bristol, Southampton or London by boat. In the twentieth century, new road networks and cars made Cornwall one of England's most popular holiday destinations. Today, holidaymakers flock to the South West and its many seaside resorts. Retired folk come here to seek peace and quiet. Artists and writers come here for inspiration. For those of us who make it our home, the South West is a very special place.

Beer Head, Devon

N 50° 41′ 06″ W 003° 05′ 38″   Map Ref: 3 L8   Grid Ref: SY228878

Sea Stacks at Ladram Bay, Devon

Dawlish Warren and Exmouth, Devon

N 50° 37' 11" W 003° 24' 24"   Map Ref: 3 J8   Grid Ref: SY005809

Salcombe, Devon

Exeter, Devon

N 50° 43' 20" W 003° 31' 40"   Map Ref: 3 I7   Grid Ref: SX922925

N 50° 41′ 58″   W 003° 48′ 23″   Map Ref: 3 G7   Grid Ref: SX725904

Castle Drogo, Devon

Haytor Rocks, Dartmoor, Devon

N 50° 35' 02" W 003° 45' 36"   Map Ref: 3 G9   Grid Ref: SX755775

Grimspound, Dartmoor, Devon

Torquay, Devon

N 50° 27' 44" W 003° 31' 22"   Map Ref: 3,110   Grid Ref: SX90636

Lynton and Lynmouth, Devon

Lundy Island, Devon

N 51° 10′ 18″ W 004° 40′ 03″   Map Ref: 3 A2   Grid Ref: SS136447

N 51° 11' 15" W 004° 13' 35"   Map Ref: 3 D2   Grid Ref: SS445455

Morte Point and the North Devon Coast, Devon

Chun Castle, Cornwall

N 50° 08' 56" W 005° 37' 55"   Map Ref: 2 D10   Grid Ref: SW406339

N 50° 09' 41" W 005° 31' 23"   Map Ref: 2 D10   Grid Ref: SW485350

Castle-an-Dinas, Cornwall

91

Merry Maidens Stone Circle, Cornwall

N 50° 03' 46" W 005° 35' 42"   Map Ref: 2 D11   Grid Ref: SW428242

Boscawen-un Stone Circle, Cornwall

Chysauster, Cornwall

N 50° 09' 56" W 005° 32' 13"   Map Ref: 2 D10   Grid Ref: SW475355

Carn Euny, Cornwall

St Michael's Mount, Cornwall

N 50° 07' 06" W 005° 28' 31"   Map Ref: 2 E10   Grid Ref: SW516300

Land's End, Cornwall

Lizard Point, Cornwall

N 49° 57′ 33″ W 005° 12′ 54″   Map Ref: 2 F12   Grid Ref: SW695115

Eastern Islands, Scilly Isles

St Mary's, Scilly Isles

Tresco, Scilly Isles

St Agnes, Scilly Isles

N 49° 53' 11" W 006° 20' 17"   Map Ref: 2 C5   Grid Ref: SV885075

N 49° 55' 51" W 006° 21' 22" Map Ref: 2 C5 Grid Ref: SV875125

Samson, Scilly Isles

St Mawes Castle, Cornwall

N 50° 09' 20" W 005° 01' 27"   Map Ref: 2 H10   Grid Ref: SW840327

N 50° 25' 26" W 004° 40' 16"   Map Ref: 2 J7   Grid Ref: SX103616

Restormel Castle, Cornwall

Tin Mine at Botallack Head, Cornwall

N 50° 08' 34" W 005° 41' 22"   Map Ref: 2 C10   Grid Ref: SW365335

Dry Stone Walls, Kenidjack, Cornwall

China Clay Quarries, Cornwall

N 50° 22' 57"   W 004° 50' 59"   Map Ref: 2 18   Grid Ref: SW977562

Eden Project, Cornwall

Tintagel, Cornwall

N 50° 40' 14" W 004° 45' 45"   Map Ref: 2 J5   Grid Ref: SX048893

Dunster Castle, Somerset

Muchelney Abbey, Somerset

N 51° 01′ 00″   W 002° 49′ 13″   Map Ref: 4 B7   Grid Ref: ST42524

Glastonbury Abbey, Somerset

Glastonbury Tor, Somerset

N 51° 08′ 37″ W 002° 41′ 41″   Map Ref. 4 C6   Grid Ref. ST515385

Wells Cathedral, Somerset

Cadbury Castle Hill Fort, Somerset

N 51° 26' 48" W 00° 46' 55" Map Ref: 4 B2 Grid Ref: ST457???

Brent Knoll, Somerset

Priddy Circles, Somerset

Priddy Barrows, Somerset

Glastonbury Festival 2003, Pilton, Somerset

N 51° 09' 59" W 002° 35' 13"   Map Ref: 4 C6   Grid Ref: ST590409

Glastonbury Festival 2003, Pilton, Somerset

Balloons over Clifton Suspension Bridge, Bristol

N 51° 27' 18" W 002° 37' 40"   Map Ref: 4 C2   Grid Ref: ST565730

N 51° 26′ 40″ W 002° 38′ 29″   Map Ref: 4 C2   Grid Ref: ST555720

Bristol Balloon Fiesta 2004, Ashton Court, Bristol

Bristol International Airport

N 51° 22' 57" W 002° 42' 50"   Map Ref: 4 C3   Grid Ref: ST504650

Bath, Somerset

Dunkery Beacon, Exmoor, Somerset

N 51° 09′ 54″ W 003° 35′ 17″   Map Ref: 3 H2   Grid Ref: SS891418

River Tone in flood, Meare Green, near Taunton, Somerset

Peat Extraction, Westhay Moor, near Glastonbury, Somerset

N 51° 09' 34" W 002° 47' 36"   Map Ref: 4 B5   Grid Ref: ST447402

Peat Extraction, Westhay Moor, near Glastonbury, Somerset

Beachy Head, East Sussex

N 50° 44' 15" E 000° 14' 41"   Map Ref: 5 J11 6 C12   Grid Ref: TV58095

IV: THE SOUTH EAST

Kent, Surrey, Sussex

South East England is the region historically most influenced by continental Europe. Since earliest times, it has been a battlefield stained by the blood of armies repelling successive invaders or engaged in civil war. Danes, Angles, Saxons, Roman legions and the army of William the Conqueror all came to invade us, the Civil War of Oliver Cromwell rebelled against an ineffectual king, and in the twentieth century, the Nazi menace caused aircrews to fight valiantly in the skies overhead, many plunging to their deaths in the fields of Kent. Today it is a gentle landscape of fields and woodlands, adorning one of the most affluent areas of Britain. To the north is London and the River Thames, while to the south, the famous white cliffs along the south east coast have been a welcoming sight for homeward bound travellers, as well as sailors, soldiers and airmen in times of war. One of the busiest waterways in the world, the English Channel, which the French call *"La Manche"* (The Sleeve) in reference to its shape, is an arm of the North Atlantic Ocean which gradually narrows towards the east to just 34 kilometres (21 miles) between Dover and Calais. Where the Strait is at its narrowest, the sea is very shallow; as little as 45 metres (132 feet) deep, making possible the Channel Tunnel, a long dreamed about project which now speeds rail passengers and freight between Britain and France.

The South East contains the North and South Downs, curved in opposing sides of an oval around the Weald, from the old English name *'wold'* for the forest that once stood there. The Downs are gently rounded hills, composed of chalk laid down on the seabed at least 120 million years ago, and the remnants of much higher mountains, pushed up some 60 million years ago by the geological upheaval of continental drift. When young they would have had jagged tops, but the soft chalk has worn away through the ages to leave gentle hills with smooth contours as we see them today.

Until about 20,000 years ago, Britain was connected to the Continent by dry land, so the first settlers in South East England arrived from Europe on foot. Skeletal remains of *Homo heidelbergensis*, some 500,000 years old, have been found at Boxgrove, in Sussex. Nearby, hand axe tools fashioned from local flint were discovered. At Swanscombe, in Kent, 400,000-years-old hand axes have been recovered from the gravels of an ancient riverbed. Part of a human skull was also found at Swanscombe showing features that suggest it could be Neanderthal and if so, it is possible that two different human species existed in Britain simultaneously.

Around 9000 BC, as the vast ice-sheets of the last Ice Age were retreating northwards, bands of Stone Age hunter-gatherers, *Homo sapiens*, occupied rock shelters in the south east of England. As the ice receded, it became warmer and by 6000 BC, temperatures had climbed to be similar to those we experience today. Where before there was treeless tundra, forests of birch and pine grew, and in time this was replaced by verdant, deciduous woodland of oak, elm and lime. The fauna changed too: elk and reindeer moved northwards with the receding tundra, while red and roe deer, along with a host of smaller mammals and birds adapted to forest living, moved in from the south. As the ice melted, the sea level rose to flood the English Channel, severing the land connection with the continent of Europe, and isolating Britain as an island. As it did so, it formed a strategically important barrier to would-be invaders, and prevented the northward migration of many animals and plants, limiting the number of species to be found in Britain.

Late neolithic settlers established their homes on the Downs, where they grew crops, kept domesticated animals, and wove cloth. They were also skilled at making tools. Polished stone axes were used to fell trees providing wood for house building and for fires. In earlier times, people had searched riverbeds, beaches and open moors for suitable stones to fashion into useful tools, but as the population grew, and new skills were developed, stone tools of many kinds were in high demand. So, they started to dig to search for good flint. Organized flint mining in the chalk happened as early as 4000 BC and at Cissbury hill fort in Sussex, some of the pits and shafts can still be seen. Mineshafts were dug down through the chalk until bands of good flint were found, then tunnels excavated horizontally outwards, using burning animal fat torches to provide light. During investigations in the 1950s, the 6,000-year-old remains of a young girl were discovered, crushed in the dark tunnel that had collapsed on her. Still clutched in her hand were the charred remains of her torch.

Bronze Age farms on the Sussex Downs around 1500 BC may have comprised four or five circular wooden huts, sometimes situated on levelled terraces. There would have been burial mounds close by and storage pits were used to keep primitive emmer wheat and hulled barley. Clay loom weights for weaving have been discovered from some of these sites - woven cloth was present in Britain well before 2000 BC, as is evident from graves where pins and cloth fasteners have been discovered. The Downs are also scattered with the remains of Iron Age hill fort settlements where the chalk proved ideal for the carving of giant hill figures as totems or landmarks. The Long Man of Wilmington hill figure in Sussex, however, is something of an enigma. At 70 metres (230 feet) long, it is reputed to be the largest representation of the human figure anywhere in the world. Many different dates have been suggested for its origin, among them Celtic, Saxon, or even Roman, but recent studies using dating techniques have suggested that it was likely created as late as the sixteenth or seventeenth centuries. There are other, even more modern hill figures in the South East, for example the Wye Crown, completed in 1902 to celebrate the coronation of King Edward VII. The most recent is the Folkestone White Horse, completed in 2003 as a millennium project. It was designed, by Charles Newington, as a symbolic landmark above the entrance to the Channel Tunnel, to celebrate Britain's Celtic heritage and new spirit as we moved into the twenty-first century.

In the third and second millennia BC, settlers travelling to Britain across the North Sea often landed on the southern edge of the Thames Estuary. Later, they came across the Dover Straits to the south coast of Kent and Sussex. The Belgae, a Celtic tribe, were the last to arrive before the Romans. They started to establish Britain's first towns, which Caesar would later call *'Oppida'* where timber houses for hundreds of people were protected by massive earthworks of banks and ditches. Julius Caesar landed at Deal in eastern Kent in 55 BC on a reconnaissance mission to forge alliances with local chiefs, returning again only a few months later, in 54 BC to penetrate further inland. He described the Belgae of Kent as sophisticated - they grew wheat, used iron ploughs with colters, and had a system of land division. Caesar dismissed the Bronze Age and Celtic peoples who lived in the interior of Britain as barbarians, but although they still wore animal skins and daubed their skin with woad - a blue dye obtained from the herb *Isatis tinctoria* - their communities throughout southern England had enjoyed considerable contact and trade links with the Continent for centuries.

Sophisticated Roman culture and exotic lifestyles had already influenced the South East via trade with the Empire on the Continent. Minerals, slaves and hunting dogs had been exported from Britain in exchange for imports of wine from Italy, fine pottery, silver and bronze ware. In AD 43, the Roman invasion came when Claudius landed at Richborough in Kent with a force of about 40,000 men. The Romans defeated the Belgae at Medway, on the Thames Estuary, but while the South East was overwhelmed without too much trouble, the conquest as a whole proved to be a long drawn-out, bloody affair. Ultimately, however, Roman customs and behaviour were to change the face of England. They built forts and roads: the first of many, Watling Street, ran from Dover to London, the road now known as the A2. They established farms and brought in craftsmen from the Continent to build sophisticated villas. They began the work of reclaiming Romney Marsh from the sea, and mined iron ore, already discovered in great quantities by Iron Age people in the Weald. Great oaks were felled and burned to produce charcoal for smelting, and the foundries supplied iron for armour and weapons, much of which was exported. The iron industry in Kent was to last until 1765, when the last forge, at Lamberhurst, closed down. Iron ore is still to be found in the Weald, however, where signs of it can be seen in the rust coloured water staining ditches along hedgerows.

The Romans destroyed huge areas of the ancient forest of the Weald, but even as late as the fourteenth century, much still survived, dense and trackless, the realm of wolves and outlaws. But the oaks would eventually be felled to supply timber for shipbuilding, and as both oak and elm became scarce, old ship timbers were reclaimed for house building. Today the Weald provides a vista of gently rolling farmland. In some areas of the South East, field patterns have remained unchanged for centuries. During late medieval times, hedges were planted as field boundaries to keep in livestock, inadvertently providing refuges and natural corridors for wild animal and plant species that had been threatened by the destruction of forests. In the last few decades, many hedges in Kent have been destroyed to create bigger fields more suited to modern farming techniques, to the detriment of wildlife.

From the sixteenth century onwards, the green belt surrounding the metropolis was fast becoming London's larder. Market gardens developed around Margate and Maidstone, with hops and fruit grown mainly to supply London. By the eighteenth century, London was demanding supplies of meat and groceries in hitherto unprecedented proportions and Kent became famous for its produce, earning it the name 'Garden of England'. Today, its orchards, hop fields and oast houses are familiar and characteristic landmarks. In 1804, rich coal seams were discovered in Kent. Exploratory mining began in 1886 near Dover, and started production in 1912. At their peak, the collieries employed over 3,000 men and produced over 800,000 tonnes of coal per annum. The last Kent coalfield closed in the 1990s.

The affluence of the South East began due to its proximity to the Continent, and only in the last millennium was it due to the influence of London, which fostered trade links throughout the world. The great wealth that resulted enabled the rich and successful to build large houses along the leafy lanes of Surrey, Kent and Sussex. Meanwhile, London spreads ever outwards in a cancerous sprawl of concrete, brick and tarmac. Already the encircling M25 motorway is failing to contain it or to provide an adequate path for relentless streams of traffic that seem to engage in an insane race to use up the last remnants of the world's fossil fuel. Many small villages in Surrey and Kent that existed as quaint backwaters fifty years ago have expanded into towns with new road systems, housing estates, supermarkets and malls. The edge of London is such a ragged mass of housing that the boundary is difficult to define. The southern parts of Surrey, however, still have the vestiges of a once beautiful countryside, although one is never, it seems, out of range of the hum of traffic, drone of aircraft, or the orange stain in the night sky reflected from urban lights.

Chichester Harbour, West Sussex

N 50° 47' 57" W 000° 55' 48"   Map Ref: 5 D10   Grid Ref: SU755005

Chichester Cathedral, West Sussex

Arundel Castle, West Sussex

N 50° 51' 57" W 000° 33' 55"   Map Ref. 5 G10   Grid Ref. TO010083

N 50° 52′ 27″   W 000° 33′ 16″   Map Ref: 5 G10   Grid Ref: 1Q01/093

Arundel Park, West Sussex

Bodiam Castle, East Sussex

N 51° 00′ 11″   E 000° 09′ 09″   Map Ref: 6 E9   Grid Ref: TV 519077

Long Man of Wilmington, East Sussex

Brighton Palace Pier, East Sussex

N 50° 48′ 55″ W 000° 08′ 16″   Map Ref: S 110   Grid Ref: TQ312034

Brighton Marina, East Sussex

White Cliffs at Beachy Head, East Sussex

N 50° 44' 15"   E 000° 14' 41"   Map Ref: 51 J1 6 C12   Grid Ref: TV 58 5955

The English Channel

Mount Caburn, East Sussex

N 50° 51' 58" E 000° 04' 20"   Map Ref: S Y10, 6 P11   Grid Ref: TQ459090

River Cuckmere at Seven Sisters, East Sussex

Herstmonceux Castle, East Sussex

Battle Abbey, East Sussex

M25/M23 Motorway Junction, Surrey

Channel Tunnel Terminal, Kent

Castle Hill, Channel Tunnel Terminal, Kent

Folkestone White Horse, Kent

Dover Castle, Kent

Dover Harbour, Kent

Leeds Castle, Kent

Allington Castle, Kent

Deal Castle, Kent

Camber Castle, East Sussex

Saltwood Castle, Kent

The Wye Crown, Kent

Canterbury Cathedral, Kent

Richborough Castle, Kent

Sissinghurst Castle, Kent

Knole House, Kent

Hever Castle, Kent

Bayham Abbey, Kent

Bewl Water, Kent

Dungeness, Kent

Rochester Castle and Cathedral, Kent

Historic Dockyard, Chatham, Kent

St Mary's Island and the Medway Estuary, Kent

Car Depository, Isle of Sheppey, Kent

Big Ben

V: LONDON

8,000 years ago, when the North Sea was dry land, the River Thames was a tributary of the River Rhine. People had been living in Britain, hunting and gathering, on and off for well over half a million years, but had made very little impact on the landscape. Prehistoric peoples must have traversed London, but evidence of their passing has mostly disappeared under layers of stone, brick, mortar and tarmac, although to the west, between Richmond and Maidenhead, stone axes have been dredged from the Thames. In London itself, on the south bank of the Thames near Vauxhall Bridge, Bronze Age wooden posts from around 1300 BC, which probably supported a causeway, have been discovered. But London did not exist as a town before AD 47, following the Roman invasion, although a small trading post had been established in AD 25 at Southwark. From here, Britons exported corn, cattle, metal and slaves to the Continent in exchange for glass and fine pottery. When the Romans invaded Britain in AD 43, they moved north eastwards from their landing place at Richborough on the Kent Coast and crossed the Thames in the London area, possibly at Lambeth, clashing with local tribesmen to the north. Some seven years later, just east of the present London Bridge, they built a wooden bridge, which became a focal point of their road system, attracting settlers and leading to London's growth as a community. Strategically, it was a good position; the River Thames was deep; boats heavily laden with trade goods could take advantage of the tides to float up and down river without being dependent on the vagaries of the wind. The area was well drained, with two hills on the north bank, Cornhill and Ludgate, offering ideal sites for habitation above the flood plain. As trade increased, the town of *'Londinium'* grew.

In AD 60, the new town was burnt to the ground by Boudicca's forces in a daring raid against Roman occupation. The town was quickly rebuilt, however, and impressive buildings, including a forum, a basilica, a bathhouse and an amphitheatre were constructed. By the second century, London already had some 20,000 inhabitants. A military fort was erected near the amphitheatre, and high stone walls were built around the city for defence. Towards the end of the third century, the Roman occupation was waning. Around AD 350, catapult towers were sited along the city walls in response to successive attacks by Picts, Scots, and Saxons. The Emperor Flavius Honorius finally renounced responsibility for Britain in AD 407. After the Romans left, London may have been virtually uninhabited for a century or more. Angles and Saxons finally recognised the strategic importance of London, however, and began to occupy an area outside the old Roman walls. Saxon King Aethelbert of Kent built the first St. Paul's Cathedral in 597, and by 640, a trading settlement began to establish itself west of the city walls. The area is now known as Aldwych, but *Lundenwic*, as it had become known by the 670s, grew into a thriving emporium. Meanwhile, the Roman city was left deserted, although a Royal Palace was eventually built in the ruins of the old Roman fort in an attempt to revive the area.

In 865, Vikings invaded East Anglia, reaching London in 871. By 878 though, Alfred the Great had become King of England and forced the Vikings to withdraw. Alfred refurbished the city's defences, repairing walls and ditches, and constructed a *south-werk* (hence the name Southwark) on the south bank of the river to protect the southern approaches. By the tenth century, London had become the most important commercial centre in England with flourishing international trade. The busy city was now full of small wooden houses and churches of stone. Viking raids continued however, and during the reign of King Aethelred, became a determined campaign to overrun Britain. By

1013, London was under siege. Viking armies took the city, and the Danish King Cnut established himself as King. In 1042, Cnut's stepson of the Saxon line was invited to take up the throne and became King Edward the Confessor. When he died, there was no obvious heir, but his cousin, Duke William of Normandy, claimed that he had been promised the English throne. The Royal Council, however, elected Edward's brother-in-law, Harold, as King, but soon after his coronation, William invaded England. Harold's army faced William's forces at Battle, near Hastings in Sussex, and lost. After his victory, William's army ravaged the country to beat the English into submission. He built the Tower of London not only to intimidate but also to protect the most important city in his new realm. By the thirteenth century, there were over 30,000 people tightly clustered along the north riverbank, with another small settlement across the river in Southwark. One of the most significant constructions of the medieval period was the replacement of the early wooden London Bridge by one built entirely of stone and featuring a drawbridge and houses along its length. It took thirty years to complete, and it was to last until 1832. St. Paul's, following a fire in 1087, had been rebuilt by the Normans who wanted to create the longest Christian church in the world. The work took more than 200 years to complete, and it was finally consecrated in 1300.

At the start of Henry VIII's reign in 1509, London was filled with splendid religious buildings, the treasures of previous centuries. During the Dissolution of the Monasteries, which began in 1538, the majority of these were destroyed or adapted for secular use. Queen Elizabeth I, who reigned 1558-1603, eventually brought more relaxed times to the people of London. It was the heyday of the English theatre, and Londoners flocked to Southwark - the entertainment centre of the city. Here were the Rose and the Globe theatres, the work places of William Shakespeare. There were also more base entertainments available such as bear baiting or cock-fighting. Then, of course, there were the brothels. Southwark was famous for its ladies of the night who worked from land belonging to the Bishop of Winchester, who regulated the industry and made himself wealthy from it.

Perhaps the most significant civic achievement of James I's reign, from 1603-1625, was the provision of a clean water supply for the capital. Before 1603, water had been piped through the hollowed out trunks of elm trees, but this had become so inadequate that a canal, called the New River, was constructed from Hertfordshire into the City to supply London with fresh water. The reign of King Charles II (1660-1685) was to experience two great disasters. The first came in 1665 when plague, a constant threat in London since medieval times, killed over 68,000 people, about a fifth of the population of the city at that time. The second followed only a year later. Early on a September morning in 1666, a baker's shop near London Bridge caught fire. It quickly spread to neighbouring houses, fanned by a wind that blew constantly for three days. By the fourth day, when the wind dropped and the fire slowly went out, the Great Fire had devastated London: only a fifth of the walled city remained unscathed; 110 hectares (273 acres) had been burned, with a total of 13,200 homes and 87 parish churches destroyed.

The fire changed the character of London forever, the new city being built with wider streets and brick houses. The devastation increased awareness of the dangers of fire and highlighted the need for new building regulations and public services. Until 1750, there was still only one bridge across the river between the City and Southwark. A second bridge was built at Westminster and only 20 years later, a third bridge was opened at Blackfriars. Soon after 1760, with around 650,000 inhabitants in London, the ancient gates and city walls were demolished. New buildings constructed during this period were opulent: Somerset House, the Bank of England, Mansion House, and Horse Guards to name only a few. Admiral Nelson's victory at the Battle of Trafalgar in 1805 achieved naval supremacy for Britain: Trafalgar Square, with Nelson's column, was created to celebrate the confidence and prosperity that resulted. In 1826, King George IV, who reigned from 1820-1830, transformed Buckingham House, his parents' London home, into the famous Royal Palace.

The construction of the railways, linking London to other major cities, transformed social and business life. Underground trains, the first in the world, and surface tram networks followed. Progress was sometimes double-edged. The invention of the modern water closet resulted in the piping of raw sewage into the Thames and, in 1833, nearly 10,000 Londoners died in a cholera epidemic. In the 'Great Stink' of 1858, pollution in the river became so bad that parliamentary sessions at Westminster had to be suspended. The construction of massive sewers followed. The Thames was seriously polluted for centuries but today it is among the cleanest of city rivers in the world.

Victorians indulged in the view that London was the centre of the world. In 1851, during Queen Victoria's reign (1837-1901), her husband Prince Albert celebrated this sense of imperial grandeur by holding a Great Exhibition in Hyde Park. He also built the Royal Albert Hall, the Victoria and Albert Museum, and the Natural History Museum. At the beginning of the twentieth century, London was a larger, busier place than it had ever been before, the centre of the world's largest empire. Electric lighting was beginning to appear, and 'horseless carriages' could occasionally be seen on the streets. There was still dire poverty though, and those who were without work had to survive on charity and scavenging.

The First World War (1914-1918) was the first in which civilians found themselves in the firing line. The Germans carried out sporadic and ineffective bombing raids using Zeppelins and Gotha (biplane) bombers. The Second World War (1939-1945), however, changed the city completely. German bombs, V-1 "doodlebugs" and V-2 rockets rained down, sometimes nightly, on London in a blitz of terrible fire and destruction, killing an estimated 43,000 civilians.

For centuries the chimneys of London had been belching smoke rich in sulphur dioxide into the atmosphere which, when mixed with rain, formed acid, seriously damaging the stonework of historic buildings. In the early 1950s, during periods of temperature inversion, London experienced a series of 'smogs', a mixture of smoke and fog, which killed significant numbers of people. They were so thick that men with lanterns were employed to walk in front of buses to guide them. The Clean Air Act of 1956, forbidding the burning of fuel that was not smokeless, gradually solved the problem.

In the late twentieth century, St Paul's and other traditional landmarks became hidden behind walls of concrete as high-rise buildings were erected. In the early 1980s, the Thames Barrier was constructed to protect London from surge tides that threatened to flood low-lying areas of the city. With a burgeoning population of over seven million inhabitants, roads and new housing developments are spreading octopus-like tentacles ever outwards into the countryside. The expanding urban area is now so big that unmeasured power and endless man-hours are consumed in moving millions of commuters to and from work. As congestion and cost threaten the quality of life, some businesses are re-locating to provincial towns, but for many, London is home like no other, a city rich in history, tradition, tragedy, and triumph, with each adding to its unique character. Everywhere there are the landmarks of its remarkable past: castles, royal palaces and timber-framed houses sit among high-rise buildings, and the infrastructure of a thriving modern metropolis.

St Paul's Cathedral

Westminster

Tower of London

Tower Bridge

Thames Barrier and Thames Sailing Barge

Thames Sailing Barge

HMS Belfast

Millennium Wheel (The London Eye)

Millennium Bridge

Albert Bridge

Hungerford Bridge & Charing Cross Station

Blackfriars Bridge

N 51° 30' 35" W 000° 05' 54"   Map Ref: 8 E6   Grid Ref: TQ320806

N 51° 30' 24" W 000° 07' 17"   Map Ref: 8 A7   Grid Ref: TQ304803

Chain of Bridges

Globe Theatre

Battersea Power Station

Buckingham Palace

Kensington Palace and Hyde Park

Albert Memorial

Royal Albert Hall

Natural History Museum

Victoria and Albert Museum

British Museum

Trafalgar Square

Oxford Circus

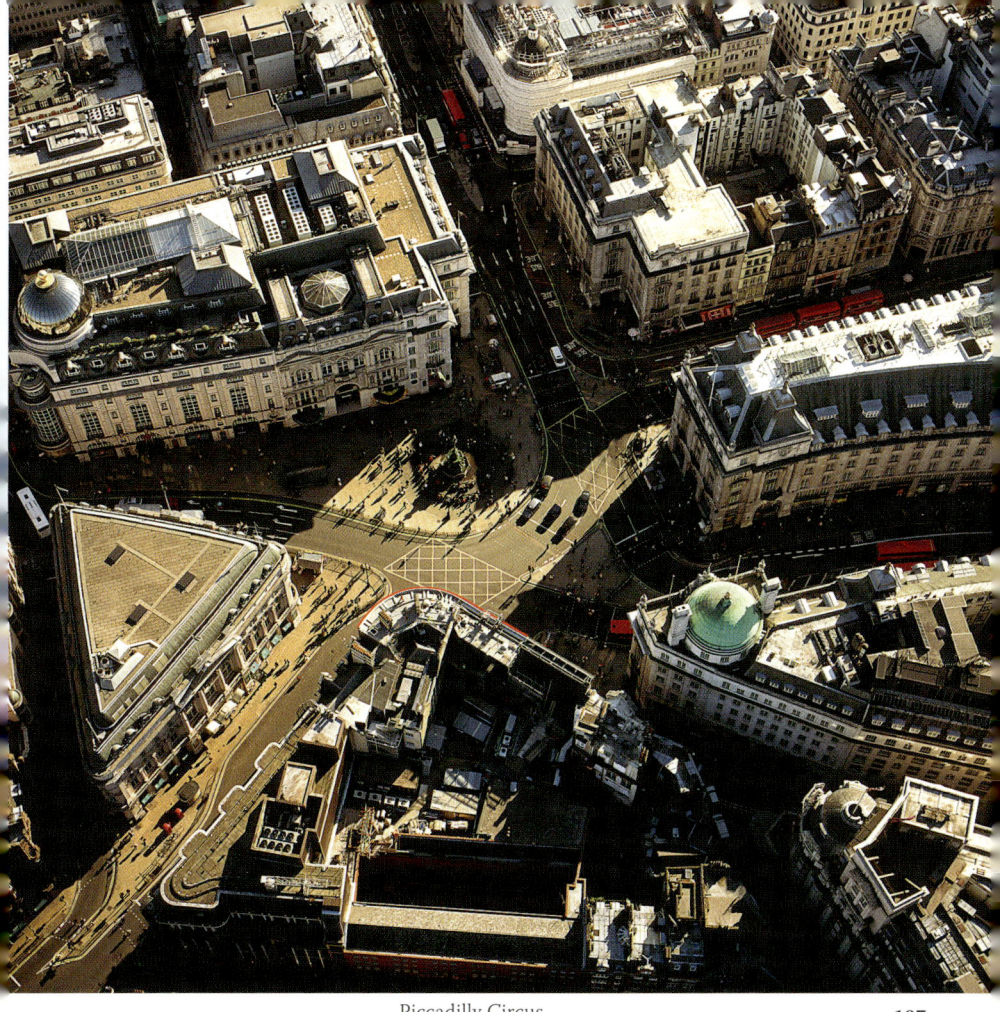

Piccadilly Circus

Covent Garden's Jubilee Arts and Crafts Market Hall

St Pancras and King's Cross Stations

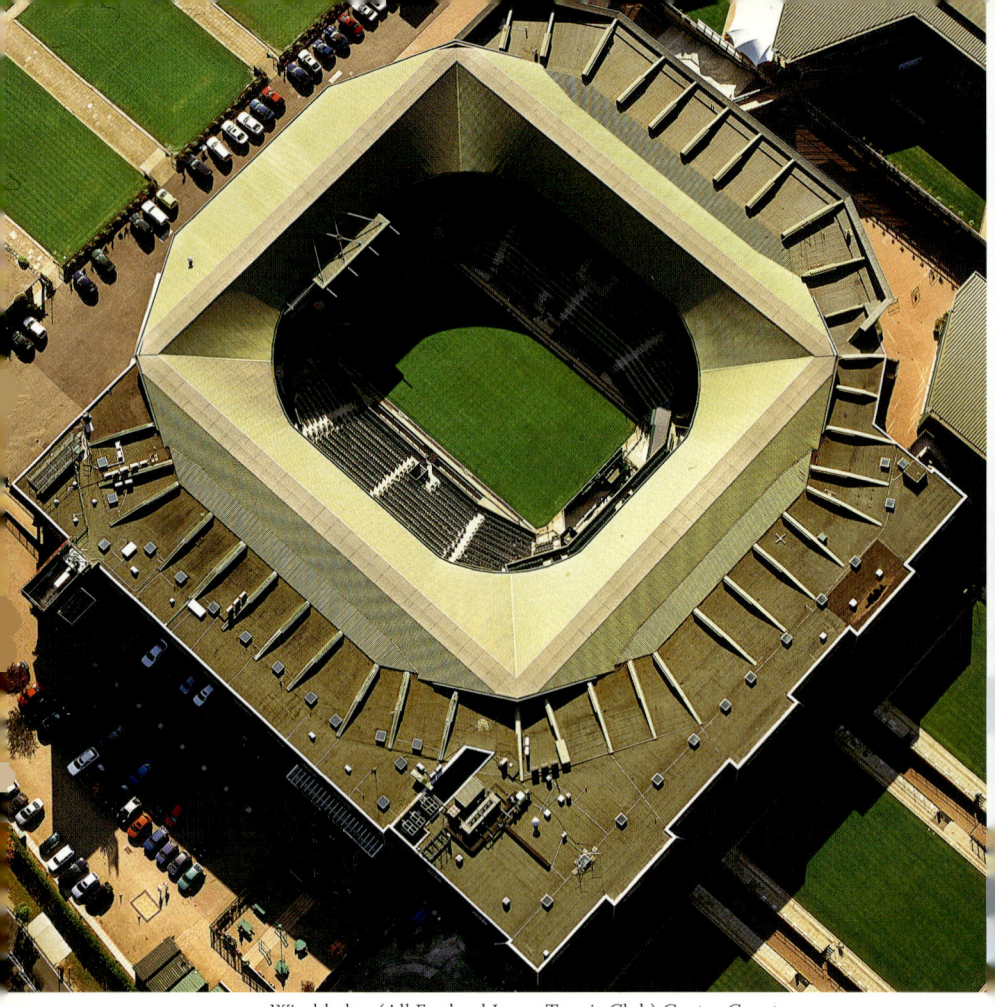

Wimbledon (All England Lawn Tennis Club) Centre Court

Lord's Cricket Ground

Greenwich

Millennium Dome

BT Tower

Old Croydon Aerodrome

One Canada Square

Canary Wharf

Swiss Re, "The Gherkin"

Tower 42 and "The Gherkin"

Oxburgh Hall, Norfolk

VI: EAST ANGLIA

Cambridgeshire, Essex, Norfolk, Suffolk

The earliest known evidence of human activity in Britain dates back 650,000 years and was found in East Anglia, predating the most extensive period of glaciations, which began about 480,000 years ago. At Happisburgh on the Norfolk coast, where the North Sea erodes the cliffs so relentlessly that the future of the village is seriously and imminently threatened, ancient layers of rock have been crumbling on to the beach. Among the Pleistocene debris, ancient palaeolithic worked flints have been discovered. At Clacton-on-Sea, in 1911, the oldest wooden artefact known in Britain, a spear about 450,000 years old was found. The people who fashioned these tools were not quite the same as us. They were *Homo heidelbergensis*, who had spread to Europe from Africa. Our own species, *Homo sapiens*, did not emerge from Africa until about 100,000 years ago. In the meantime, Neanderthals, *Homo neanderthalensis*, had already evolved in Europe, surviving until about 30,000 years ago. The land link between Britain and the Continent was finally broken by 5900 BC, having become gradually inundated over three millennia. The last section to be flooded was along the Norfolk coast and by 4900 BC, the coastline of Britain had assumed its modern shape.

Early settlers arriving in East Anglia followed a route that swept northwards from the North Downs, across southern Cambridgeshire. Parts of this track later became the Icknield Way, named for the Iceni tribe who used it to trade with people living in other parts of Britain. During the late neolithic period from 2700-2000 BC, flint was mined for manufacturing tools and weapons at Grimes Graves near Brandon, in Norfolk. As in Boxgrove, West Sussex, pits were dug into the chalk with radiating tunnels following the course of the layers of flint. Some of the tunnels are so small that only children could have crawled through them, using antlers from red deer as mining tools. Flint tools continued to be used throughout the Bronze Age; the transitions to bronze, and later to iron, did not happen overnight. At Holme-next-the-Sea in Norfolk, the shifting sands of the North Sea have exposed several Bronze Age sites, among them Seahenge, a ring of fifty-five oak timbers with a central upturned oak root, which is over 4,050 years old.

At the time of the Roman conquest, the Celtic Iceni tribe inhabited what we now know as Norfolk and parts of Suffolk. The Roman occupation brought about unwelcome changes to the old tribal way of life. The Romans conscripted young Britons into the Empire's army and treated them as slave labour to help build towns, roads, forts and country villas. In AD 60, Prasutagus, who was king of the Iceni, died. With no male heir, he left his wealth to his wife Boudicca, his two daughters and to the Roman Emperor Nero, expecting in return imperial protection for his tribe. Instead, the Romans annexed his kingdom, and humiliated the family. In fury, Boudicca allied the Iceni with the Trinovantes of Essex to form a formidable, rebellious force. In one of the bloodiest revolts in British history, thousands of Britons overran and burned the Romans' main colony at *Camulodunum* (Colchester) before doing the same to London and *Verulamium* (St Albans). They killed some 70,000 Romans along with members of the pro-Roman British tribe, the Catuvellauni. In reprisal, the provincial governor Suetonius Paulinus lured the Britons into a pitched battle near what is now Fenny Stratford, where the Romans' superior military techniques gained them a bloody victory. Boudicca is said to have taken her own life.

Following the collapse of the Roman Empire, Britain was settled by a continuous flow of people, predominantly Angles and Saxons. By the sixth century, England (land of the Angles) was really a series of separate kingdoms, each with its own royal dynasty. The kings of East Anglia were known as '*Wuffings*,' after Wuffa, the first king, who reigned from AD 571 to 578. His grandson Redwald is almost certainly the king whose magnificent ship burial was discovered at Sutton Hoo, near Ipswich, in 1939. The last was Edmund, who became king in AD 855 aged only fifteen, and in 870 faced Danish Viking invaders, who were moving through the countryside destroying everything in their path. They offered King Edmund peace on condition that he would give up his power and forbid the practice of Christianity. Edmund refused, fought, was captured and murdered. His burial place is the town of Bury St. Edmunds, in Suffolk. King Alfred of Wessex halted the advance of the Danes in 878 by defeating them at the Battle of Ethandune (believed to be Edington in Wiltshire). Under the terms of the resulting Treaty of Wedmore, in Somerset, the Danes were obliged to withdraw to a line north and east of Watling Street, the old Roman road. The Danes, however, continued to harass Wessex until Edward the Elder finally defeated them in 917. After that, East Anglia became reunited with England.

As the ports of Yarmouth and King's Lynn were established, East Anglia became one of the most densely populated regions in Britain. Forest was cleared to create agricultural land and the economic centre shifted to Norwich. In Iceni and early Saxon times, Thetford had been the capital of East Anglia. By the Norman Conquest, all of East Anglia's towns and most of its present-day villages were already in existence. The Normans encountered resistance fighters in East Anglia, led by Hereward the Wake, who attacked and sacked Peterborough Abbey but was finally beaten at the Isle of Ely. The architectural legacy of the Norman Conquest is significant. The hurriedly built early wooden castles were systematically replaced by impressive and formidable stone structures. Castle Rising in Norfolk, and Framlingham Castle in Suffolk were both built during the twelfth century. Norwich, in 1150, was one of the largest towns in England, and King's Lynn had grown to become the fifth largest port. Huge flocks of sheep were farmed for the prosperous wool industry that had been started by the Romans. From the fourteenth century the manufacture of fine worsted cloth, which took its name from the village of Worstead, developed. The Black Death of 1349 reduced the population of East Anglia dramatically, and many medieval villages either shrank or were abandoned altogether. Sometimes an isolated church is a clue to a deserted village, for example at Pudding Norton, near Fakenham, in Norfolk. Over a hundred Norfolk villages that were mentioned in the Domesday Book had disappeared by the year 1500, and the Black Death was to remain a recurring menace.

The wealth that came to East Anglia from the wool trade enabled the building of many magnificent country houses. Together with the lavish ornamental landscapes and formal gardens that surround them, they make a characteristic and prominent feature in the landscape. Perhaps the best known is Sandringham, in Norfolk, which has been the private home for four generations of sovereigns since 1862. Her Majesty Queen Elizabeth and other members of the royal family regularly spend Christmas there. The grounds at Holkham Hall, in Norfolk, are extensive, landscaped in the eighteenth century by Capability Brown, who created a lake and planted thousands of trees. One of the oldest of the great houses is Oxburgh Hall, in Norfolk, a manor built in 1482 in the style of a castle, complete with a moat.

The period from 1780 to 1880 saw many changes in England. Due to the Industrial Revolution, the population tripled. In urban areas, it increased by up to 40 per cent in only ten years. Pressure was placed on farmers to produce more food so innovative techniques had to be found to increase crop yields. Thomas Coke of Norfolk, Earl of

Leicester, gathered together farmers and friends with an interest in agricultural reform at Holkham Hall. The meetings became known as "Holkham Shearings" and helped to find solutions to make England self-sufficient. Common land was given over to cultivation; open farming methods were enclosed by hedges and fences, and a system of crop rotation was introduced to give the soil a chance to recover between harvests. These methods had the desired effect, although in the 1790s a run of poor harvests, combined with import restrictions imposed due to the Napoleonic Wars, led to desperate measures. Bread had to be made using inferior wheat and other ingredients such as beans, peas and acorns. The situation improved during the nineteenth century, aided by the growth of the railways, which helped distribution of produce to the markets. Today, modern farming methods have changed the landscape yet again. Small farms have been absorbed into larger units. Hedges have been cut and ditches filled in to create huge fields that are served by powerful tractors and combine harvesters. Vast crop monocultures result in deserts for wildlife, and the destruction of hedgerows removes the corridors and refuges that provide precious habitats for wild plants, small animals and birds. The Second World War dramatically changed the landscape of East Anglia too, with the building of huge airfields, some of which remain today as military airbases for the United States Air Force.

Today, Norfolk ('North Folk') is the largest and least populated county in East Anglia. The northern part is fenland, bordering on to the Wash and the North Sea; a rich, dark land beneath a huge sky, much of it below sea level and crisscrossed by networks of water channels that drain into the Wash, a huge shallow bay with havens for birds on the mudflats, salt marshes and tidal inlets. Norfolk's cathedral city, Norwich, is East Anglia's cultural and metropolitan centre. To the east are the Norfolk Broads, wide expanses of water trapped in hollows formed by centuries of peat extraction for use as fuel for heating and cooking purposes. Cuts were made to join the lakes to several rivers creating a network of broads, and meandering channels, which are popular among boating enthusiasts. Beds of reeds are grown along their edges for thatching Norfolk's charming country cottages.

To the south of Norfolk is Suffolk ('South Folk'), the easternmost county in England. Here, pastoral scenes of quintessential English countryside along the River Stour have been recorded for posterity by artists Thomas Gainsborough (1727-1788) and John Constable (1776-1837). To the west is Cambridgeshire, a mixture of gentle, low-lying uplands or 'isles' set in flat fenland with dead straight roads. It is renowned for its broad expanses of cereal crops on the uplands and potatoes from the Fens. In the past, the watery landscape provided conditions for famous local industries such as basket weaving and papermaking. The beautiful city of Cambridge, in Cambridgeshire, is famous for its fine architecture and is home to Cambridge University, one of the oldest universities in the world. The colleges are arranged along a stretch of water known as the "Backs", among them King's College, founded in 1441 by King Henry VI, with its famous chapel and the largest fan-vaulted ceiling in the world, and Trinity College, Cambridge's largest college, founded in 1546 by King Henry VIII.

The south coast of Essex (East Saxons) follows the north bank of the Thames Estuary. *Camulodunum* (Colchester) was the old Roman capital, and is the oldest recorded town in England. London has overflowed into Essex, together with over a million new inhabitants, in the fastest growing population expansion anywhere in Britain. It started during the latter part of the nineteenth century and has increased steadily ever since. Ribbon development, the building of houses along the main roads, has been followed by fill-in development. Housing estates, high-rise blocks, supermarkets and garages are now swallowing up the last remnants of rural landscape between the roads. The once quiet country lanes of Essex now carry solid unrelenting streams of traffic.

Thetford Priory, Norfolk

Castle Rising, Norfolk

Sandringham, Norfolk

Holkham Hall, Norfolk

Norwich Cathedral, Norfolk

Castle Acre Castle, Norfolk

Blakeney Point, Norfolk

Blakeney Point, Norfolk

Norton Creek and Overy Marsh, Norfolk

Northey Island on the River Blackwater, Maldon, Essex

The Broads at Ludham Bridge, Norfolk

New and Old Bedford Rivers on the Fens near Mepal, Cambridgeshire

Orford Beach, Suffolk

Orford Castle, Suffolk

Ickworth House, Suffolk

Framlingham Castle, Suffolk

Somerleyton Hall, Suffolk

Yew Hedge Maze at Somerleyton Hall, Suffolk

231

Martello Tower at Aldeburgh, Suffolk

Duxford Aerodrome, Cambridgeshire

Peterborough Cathedral, Cambridgeshire

Ely Cathedral, Cambridgeshire

Cambridge University and "The Backs", Cambridgeshire

Elton Hall, Cambridgeshire

American War Cemetery, Madingley, Cambridgeshire

Hadleigh Castle, Essex

Colchester Castle, Essex

Castle Hedingham, Essex

M25/M11 Motorway Junction, Essex

West Mersea, Essex

Southend-on-Sea Pier, Essex

Thames Haven, Essex

River Thames at Swinford, Oxfordshire

VII: THE WEST AND EAST MIDLANDS

Bedfordshire, Buckinghamshire, Gloucestershire, Greater Birmingham, Herefordshire, Hertfordshire, Northamptonshire, Oxfordshire, Warwickshire, Worcestershire

The West and East Midlands cover a broad swathe of Central England, from the Welsh border in the west, following the line of the River Thames in the south, and extending to East Anglia in the east. Greater Birmingham, itself now rather confusingly known as West Midlands, is thriving, prosperous, and Britain's second largest city. By the middle of the sixteenth century, Birmingham was already developing an industrial reputation making horseshoes and weaponry for the Royal Army. By the nineteenth century, during the Industrial Revolution, it was one of the great workshops of the world, although soiled by pollution that encrusted the city in tar and filth. While it brought wealth and prosperity for some, for others it brought devastating poverty and disease. To the west of Birmingham, spilling into Staffordshire and Worcestershire, is the area traditionally known as the 'Black Country', the name it gained in the nineteenth century from the smoke belching forth from hundreds of ironworking foundries, and from the dark heaps of spoil from coalmines that littered the countryside. While the Midlands still have a reputation for huge urban and industrial conurbations, some of the finest rural landscapes in England are to be found here.

Worcestershire extends southwards from the industrial fringes of Greater Birmingham to the rural England of the famous Cotswold and Malvern Hills. The Cotswolds reach a height of nearly 300 metres (984 feet), extending from Gloucestershire north eastward through six counties almost as far as the city of Oxford. The attractive mellow colour of Cotswold stone distinguishes the villages and small towns, which blend beautifully into the landscape. The area became very prosperous from the wool trade in the Middle Ages and has remained affluent for centuries, since Cotswold country is particularly suitable for sheep grazing. Some of the wealth was used to build large, elaborate churches. Even back in Roman times, the Cotswolds were intensively farmed, and villas, such as the fine example at Chedworth near Cirencester, were built from the distinctive mellow stone and decorated with beautiful mosaic floors. The highest peak in the Malverns is Worcestershire Beacon at 425 metres (1,394 feet), and there are several prehistoric sites of interest, including Herefordshire Beacon, a spectacular Iron Age Hill Fort that may be the place where the Celtic leader Caractacus was captured by the Romans. The rock composing the Malverns is very ancient, formed from 600 million-years-old Pre-Cambrian granite, which holds immense quantities of rainwater that filters through to emerge as pure natural spring water. People visited Malvern for its spring water as early as 1622, and it was bottled and marketed from 1856. Today, Malvern water is famous worldwide with over 12 million litres bottled and sold annually.

Herefordshire extends westwards to the rugged landscapes of Wales. The Welsh border was known as the "Marches", the scene of border struggles between Anglo-Saxons and the Welsh, and then between Norman Lords and Welsh Princes. The conflicts left marks on the landscape in the form of earthwork fortifications and stone castles. Today, Herefordshire is known for its cider orchards and hops, and is the birthplace of the Hereford breed of cattle. The Cathedral in Hereford houses one of Britain's finest chained libraries, and the world-famous Mappa Mundi, a medieval treasure which reveals how thirteenth century scholars interpreted the world.

To the south of Herefordshire, Gloucestershire stretches from the Welsh border eastwards, across the ancient Forest of Dean and the River Severn to the Cotswold Hills. Further east still, Warwickshire is famous as the birthplace of William Shakespeare, and boasts two of the country's most spectacular medieval castles, at Warwick and at Kenilworth. Throughout this area are many deserted medieval villages and fine examples of ancient ridge-and-furrow plough marks. The villages were abandoned either because of the Black Death, or because wealthy yeomen of the emerging middle class, during the fifteenth to seventeenth centuries, forcibly evicted villagers to take over the land. Oxfordshire is renowned for the famous university at Oxford, the oldest in the English-speaking world and thought by some to have been founded by King Alfred the Great in the ninth century. In Saxon times, schools were associated with the monastic foundation of St. Frideswide, founded around AD 700 on the site of Christ Church, which later grew as Oxford University. By 1167, after King Henry II forbade English students from studying at Paris, large numbers of scholars were in residence at Oxford. Over the centuries, the University has produced 4 British Kings, 47 Nobel Prize winners, 25 British Prime Ministers, and 6 Saints.

To the south west of Oxford, and south of the Thames, is the Vale of the White Horse. Of all the giant hill figures cut into the chalk hills of England, the white horse at Uffington is perhaps the most famous. It is certainly the oldest and by far the biggest, at 110 metres (360 feet) long. The artistic style of the horse is bold and impressionistic, and although the shape must have altered through time and periodic maintenance, similar images are known to have appeared on Late Iron Age coins. As with many of the hill figures, it is associated with an Iron Age hill fort, known as Uffington Castle, which dates back to around 700 BC. Accurate dating of hill figures is difficult since the surface of the soil is regularly disturbed during the periodic maintenance required to prevent them from disappearing under new turf. However, a research technique called Optically Stimulated Luminescence, which measures the length of time buried soil has been shut away from sunlight, suggested an origin for the horse of between 1400 and 600 BC, closely matching the age of the hill fort. Northamptonshire, Buckinghamshire, Bedfordshire and Hertfordshire, a block of four counties lying to the north and west of London, were once densely forested but are now primarily agricultural, although encroached upon by London's sprawling commuter belt.

During the Pleistocene, until the onset of glaciations around 480,000 years ago, the early River Thames flowed from present-day Wales to Clacton-on-Sea. Today, the river rises in the Cotswold Hills, in Gloucestershire, but there is more than one contender for the source. The official one is "Thames Head", in the parish of Coates, south west of Cirencester, not far from the Roman road called the Fosse Way, in a field called Trewsbury Mead. There an ancient ash tree grows by a stony hollow in the ground from which the river springs to flow down a sloping meadow at the beginning of its long journey to the North Sea. Unofficially, the Thames rises at Seven Springs, in the parish of Coberley, a few miles to the north west of the official source. Here, in a hollow by a busy road, a small stream appears briefly from its underground passage and there is even a stone with an inscription in Latin, which reads: "*Hic tuus o pater Tamesine septemgeminus fons*". Seven Springs is higher than Thames Head, and is further from the estuary, adding some 14.5 kilometres (9 miles) to the official length of the river, which is 346 kilometres (215 miles). The Thames flows eastwards from the Cotswolds towards Oxford, where it is called the Isis, a truncation of its Roman name *Thamesis*. From there, it continues on to London where the river becomes tidal as the North Sea begins to affect its flow. While this change of flow would have been helpful to boats carrying cargo upriver a few centuries ago, it also brought floods when heavy rain, combined with powerful spring tides caused high river spates. The water flow was gradually controlled by a system of weirs and locks and, more recently, by the Thames

Barrier downstream from the City of London.

Throughout history, the river has been a highway, but it was also an effective barrier. Crossing points, whether they were bridges or fords, were important not only for travelers but from a strategic military point of view. By the end of the seventh century, the shallowness of the Thames at Oxford (from the Anglo-Saxon *'Oxenaforda,'* meaning a ford for oxen) made it a natural crossing place for people traveling between the Midlands and trading centres on the south coast. There were several other crossing places in Oxfordshire: Wallingford was the site of a ford; the Romans probably settled here, and the Anglo-Saxons certainly did. Upstream, at Swinford, where the river meanders through lush green meadows, there has been a crossing for close on 1,000 years. Originally, it was a ford for pigs, hence the name *'swine ford.'* At Radcot, where the Thames divides into three channels around two small islands, is the oldest bridge on the river, which carries the old north-south road from Mercia to Wessex. Over the centuries, there have been many bloody clashes to control this ancient crossing place. Here, in 1141, King Stephen defeated the forces of his cousin Matilda, Empress of Anjou, who was campaigning to depose him. She had built an earthwork fortification just to the north of the bridge, the remains of which are still quite clearly defined.

Officially, the Thames is not the longest river in Great Britain, a title that belongs to the River Severn, which is 354 kilometres (221 miles) long. It rises in the Cambrian Mountains in Wales, before passing through Shropshire, Worcestershire and Gloucestershire on its way south to the Bristol Channel. There, two impressive modern bridges link Wales with the southern counties of England. The river is famous for a tidal phenomenon known as the "Severn Bore". The Severn estuary has the second largest tidal range in the world after the Bay of Fundy in Canada, at around 15 metres (50 feet). The shape of the estuary is like a funnel, so at high tide, the rising water is therefore forced into a narrowing channel creating a wave, the Severn Bore, that travels rapidly upstream against the river current. Between the River Severn and the scenically beautiful River Wye, lies the Forest of Dean, one of the ancient forests in England. The Romans exploited its natural resources, especially iron ore, but also timber, which they used to make charcoal for smelting, just as the Celts had done before them since 450 BC. The forest became a nationally important area for iron production for centuries, and its timber was used to build ships. Later, deposits of coal were discovered, and were mined until the 1980s.

The major historical event that was to change the landscape in the West and East Midlands was the Industrial Revolution. The ancient Forest of Arden once covered much of the land now occupied by Birmingham's urban sprawl, but it was ruthlessly cut in the eighteenth and nineteenth centuries to provide fuel for growing industries. The coalfields of nearby northern Warwickshire were among the most productive in the country, and greatly enhanced the industrial growth of Birmingham. But, as industries developed, there was one major difficulty – the transportation of raw materials to the hubs of industry, and the distribution of manufactured goods around the country, or to the ports for export. The building of canals initially solved the problem and grew rapidly in importance, expanding into a complex network of waterways. The building of railways led to the demise of the canal system as a means for transporting goods, and the development of roads during the twentieth century brought about a sudden leap in mass urbanisation that resulted in the landscape we live in today. This expansion is bound to continue, until the combined forces of dwindling natural resources and congestion define the limits beyond which the future of our continuing survival rests.

Uffington White Horse, Oxfordshire

Uffington Castle Hill Fort, Oxfordshire

River Thames, downstream from Lechlade, Gloucestershire

River Thames, Clifton Hampden, Oxfordshire

River Thames, north-west of Pangbourne, Oxfordshire

River Thames, North Stoke, Oxfordshire

River Thames between Shiplake (Oxfordshire) and Wargrave (Berkshire)

River Thames at Temple Island, near Henley-on-Thames, Oxfordshire

River Thames at Mapledurham, Oxfordshire

River Thames at Marlow, Buckinghamshire

Didcot Power Station, Oxfordshire

Oxford, Oxfordshire

St Albans Cathedral, Hertfordshire

Compton Wynyates, Warwickshire

Warwick Castle, Warwickshire

Kenilworth Castle, Warwickshire

Deserted Village, Middle Ditchford, Gloucestershire

Sudeley Castle, Gloucestershire

Sodbury Camp Hill Fort, Gloucestershire

Forest of Dean, Gloucestershire

Second Severn Bridge, Gloucestershire

Golden Valley, Herefordshire

Spaghetti Junction, West Midlands

Coventry Cathedral, West Midlands

Dudley Castle, West Midlands

Maze at Stucton's Heath, Worcestershire

Witley Court, Worcestershire

The Abberley Hall Clock Tower, Worcestershire

Great Malvern, Worcestershire

Herefordshire Beacon, Worcestershire

Potteries at Stoke-on-Trent, Staffordshire

VIII: THE NORTH MIDLANDS

Derbyshire, Leicestershire, Lincolnshire,
Nottinghamshire, Shropshire, Staffordshire

The cradle of industry that changed the face of England during the eighteenth and nineteenth centuries is to be found in one of England's most rural counties. At Coalbrookdale in Shropshire, in 1709, a technique for smelting iron, using coke, was invented by Abraham Darby. It marked the beginning of the Industrial Revolution that, for a while, placed Britain ahead of every other country in the world. It changed not only a handicraft and agricultural economy to one dominated by machinery, but our whole way of life. Shropshire held all the materials needed for industrial development. The county is a geological paradise, containing just about every rock type and mineral to be found anywhere in northern Europe. The Ironbridge Gorge is a deep natural valley, cut by the floodwaters from retreating ice at the end of the last Ice Age. In the gorge, seams of coal and iron ore, combined with a plentiful supply of wood, and waterpower provided by the River Severn, meant that everything was available in one spot. For decades, smoke and fumes filled the gorge from the many kilns, furnaces and factories that were constructed along its base. The world's first cast iron bridge, built across the gorge at Coalbrookdale in 1779, became a lasting symbol of industrial achievement.

New manufacturing techniques were invented throughout the Midlands, using innovative energy sources and new materials, increasing efficiency and making possible the mass production of goods in factories. The Industrial Revolution led to new developments in transportation, from steam locomotion to the internal combustion engine. It also encouraged the reorganization of agriculture, where greater productivity was needed to provide enough food for an increasingly non-agricultural population. The industrialisation of agriculture, using machines to do the work previously undertaken by farm labourers, led to larger field sizes and the amalgamation of smallholdings. A massive cultural and geographical transformation took place as people moved from the countryside to the cities. Until that time, Stoke-on-Trent, in Staffordshire, was a small village, one of many collectively known as 'The Potteries'. Excavations in the area have revealed pottery from the Bronze Age around 1700 BC, and some fine pieces from the Roman occupation. In the seventeenth century, potters were criticised for digging holes in the roads to obtain clay - a habit that gave rise to the term 'potholes'. By 1800, when the Industrial Revolution was in full spate, nearby villages merged with Stoke-on-Trent to form the largest pottery manufacturing centre in the world, and many of the great manufacturing names like Wedgwood, Minton, and Spode came from here. Pollution, however, was a major problem because of the large number of pottery kilns, and remained so until as recently as the 1950s. It was not uncommon for the sun to be virtually blacked out by the smoke, and the area was infamous for a high death rate associated with lung disease.

Further south, in the Staffordshire Black Country, the intensive exploitation of coal and iron ore during the eighteenth and nineteenth centuries led to a pollution-encrusted industrial landscape. Collieries, blast furnaces and iron foundries pumped pungent smoke and grime into the atmosphere, coating buildings for miles around with filth. Today, modern industrial methods no longer produce such extreme pollution, but the past has left indelible scars in spoil heaps and abandoned industrial sites. Elsewhere too, even in rural Shropshire, sterile grey waste, old shafts and crumbling buildings are a reminder of the lead mining days. The biggest lead mine in Shropshire was at Snailbeach, and it is reputed to have yielded the greatest volume of lead per acre of any mine in Europe. Mining activities there date from Roman times and continued until 1955. A Roman lead ingot, weighing almost 90 kilograms (193 lb), with *"IMP HADRIANI AVG"* (Emperor Hadrian Augustus) engraved on it, was found there in 1796.

The Black Country is separated from the potteries of the north by an oasis of forest and heath. Cannock Chase includes the last remnant of the ancient oak forest of Cannock and is the northernmost example of a lowland heath habitat in Britain, although much of it is now covered by conifer plantations of larch, spruce and pine, planted by the Forestry Commission. The famous Sherwood Forest of Robin Hood, in Nottinghamshire, has few of its grand old oaks or beeches left. Much of Charnwood Forest, in Leicestershire, has been cleared to make way for quarrying activities. Most of these woodlands are the remnants of ancient forests that were, for centuries, royal preserves for hunting deer and wild boar.

The high moorlands of the Peak District National Park in Derbyshire comprise some of England's most attractive hill scenery. An upland plateau, some 50 kilometres (30 miles) long and 35 kilometres (22 miles) wide, it forms the southern section of the Pennines between Sheffield and Manchester. The highest peak is Kinderscout, at 636 metres (2,088 feet). In winter, it can be bleak, though wonderfully wild and remote. It became Britain's first National Park in 1950, and the first long-distance footpath in Britain was the Pennine Way, which starts from the village of Edale. The Peak District was formed from the sediments, in places over 600 metres (2,000 feet) thick, from coral atolls and tropical lagoons, when Britain was situated just south of the Equator more than 300 million years ago. Pollen samples from peat bogs in the Peaks show that, at the end of the last Ice Age, parts of the area became densely wooded. On higher ground to the north and west, the trees gave way to light scrub cover dominated by birch and juniper. The felling of trees, combined with a warm, wet climate some 7,000 years ago, contributed to extensive peat formation.

Early settlements in the Peak District are mostly known from scattered discoveries of stone tools, and chambered barrows dating back to the early neolithic period. Burial barrows were usually built in prominent places where the living could be constantly reminded of their ancestors. Between 3000 and 2000 BC, two large henges were constructed. One is on the limestone plateau at Arbor Low, overlooking a valley to the west, while the Bull Ring, near Buxton, sits at the bottom of a valley. At henges such as these, people from local communities would gather for rituals, to exchange gifts and to feast. There are several hill forts in the Peak District, some of which may have only been seasonally occupied to be near good pasture for livestock, but Mam Tor was a large settlement which, judging from the shallow platforms inside it, contained many dwellings.

In the Peak District, from the early Bronze Age to the late Iron Age, areas were cleared of stones to create small, irregular fields. Cultivation was then undertaken using wooden tools to grow cereal crops, while sheep and cattle were pastured nearby on open ground. During the Roman occupation, and much later, in the eleventh and thirteenth centuries, there were long periods of good climate. Farming flourished and vineyards were established as far north as Yorkshire. In the fourteenth century, the weather became wetter and colder, and this, combined with the spread of the Black Death in 1348-9, caused the cultivation of crops to decline. Plague kept recurring throughout England for over three hundred years. The tragic story of self-sacrifice in the village of Eyam, in the Hope Valley, is not unique. In September 1665, a tailor who lived in the village was sent some cloth from London, but the material was infected with plague and he died a few days later. The disease quickly spread but the Rector persuaded the people to stay in an attempt to prevent the infection from spreading to other communities. In just over a year, out of a population of just over 300, 257 villagers died. The victims were hurriedly interred in graves scattered around the village, usually without any funeral ceremony, to reduce the risk of infection. During their year of isolation, food was left for the village high up on the hill, paid for by coins dipped in vinegar to disinfect them.

The counties of the North Midlands are known for dairy farming, sheep and the cultivation of cereal crops. In Staffordshire, the water meadows of the River Dove make excellent dairy farming country. In Leicestershire, the rich farmland is in the uplands of the east and is famous for its Stilton cheese. Derbyshire is known for its market gardening, and Lincolnshire for its commercial bulb growing industry. The reclaimed fenland of Lincolnshire and Nottinghamshire is very fertile with thick layers of dark peat. Drainage of the fens began in Roman times and some of the canals and dykes, notably Foss Dyke, date back to the occupation. The Romans named Lincolnshire *Lindum Colonia*: a colony for retired soldiers. Lincoln is the only city in England where it is still possible to drive through a Roman gateway. In the Second World War, Lincolnshire was known as "Bomber County", with thousands of aircraft flying out of scores of bases to bomb the Third Reich. Some still remain active as military airfields, while most have been reclaimed as agricultural land, often with just the remains of lonely control towers to remind us of the thousands of airmen who lost their lives on missions from which they never returned.

The western border of Shropshire meets the wild, hilly landscapes of Wales. A linear earthwork, consisting of a ditch and a rampart called Offa's Dyke, follows the ancient boundary with Wales for some 224 kilometres (140 miles). It was constructed during the reign of Offa, King of Mercia, in the eighth century and carefully positioned to allow clear views into Wales along its length. Border wars between the Welsh and the English were chronic, so the dyke was a military boundary and must have been a massive undertaking to create. For much of its length, it is still visible, although parts of it have vanished beneath centuries of ploughing. The Welsh resisted conquest through guerrilla warfare, carrying out raids across the border by moving swiftly and secretly along mountain trails. William the Conqueror tried to control the Welsh by setting up border earldoms, which became known as the Marches, with castles built in strategic positions. Ludlow Castle was built some time after 1086, as the principal stronghold, on a cliff overlooking the River Teme.

In eastern Derbyshire, near the Nottinghamshire border, the first known example of palaeolithic cave art ever to be found in England lies in the caves of Creswell Crags, a limestone gorge. The artwork, which shows ibex, bison, horses, birds and geometric patterns, dates back to between 50,000 and 10,000 years ago, when people occupied the site to hunt mammoth, reindeer, and woolly rhinoceros. Back then, people led very simple lives and it was much later that we learned how to shape the landscape to provide for our needs. Later still came the ability to change the landscape on a grander scale, not only for necessity but for status, as can be seen in the many stately homes that grace the English countryside. Nowhere in England is this more evident than in the Midlands. During the fashionable sixteenth century, Chatsworth House, Haddon Hall and Hardwick Hall, all in Derbyshire, were built or lavishly altered on a grand scale by an elite group of families who wielded great power. As a group, they were even more powerful than the king, their collective influence based on the ownership of land and great wealth. Today, the wealthiest are the entrepreneurs of industry and business. Our cities are now so large that they have begun to merge one with another, linked by networks of fast moving transportation that threaten to smother the land. Meanwhile, the grand houses and the ancient sites, at which we gaze in awe and fascination, remain as ghosts of the past.

Ironbridge, Shropshire

Ironbridge Power Station, Shropshire

Ludlow Castle, Shropshire

Stokesay Castle, Shropshire

Wroxeter Roman Town, Shropshire

Atcham Bridge, Shropshire

Church Stretton, Shropshire

Lichfield Cathedral, Staffordshire

Stafford Castle, Staffordshire

Tutbury Castle, Staffordshire

Cannock Chase, Staffordshire

Ridge and Furrow Ploughmarks by the River Dove, near Uttoxeter, Staffordshire

Alton Castle, Staffordshire

Alton Towers Funfair, Staffordshire

Chatsworth House, Derbyshire

Hardwick Hall, Derbyshire

Edge of Peak District, near Kettleshulme, Derbyshire

Derwent Reservoir, Peak District, Derbyshire

Howden Reservoir, Peak District, Derbyshire

Ladybower Reservoir, Peak District, Derbyshire

Alport Dale, Derbyshire

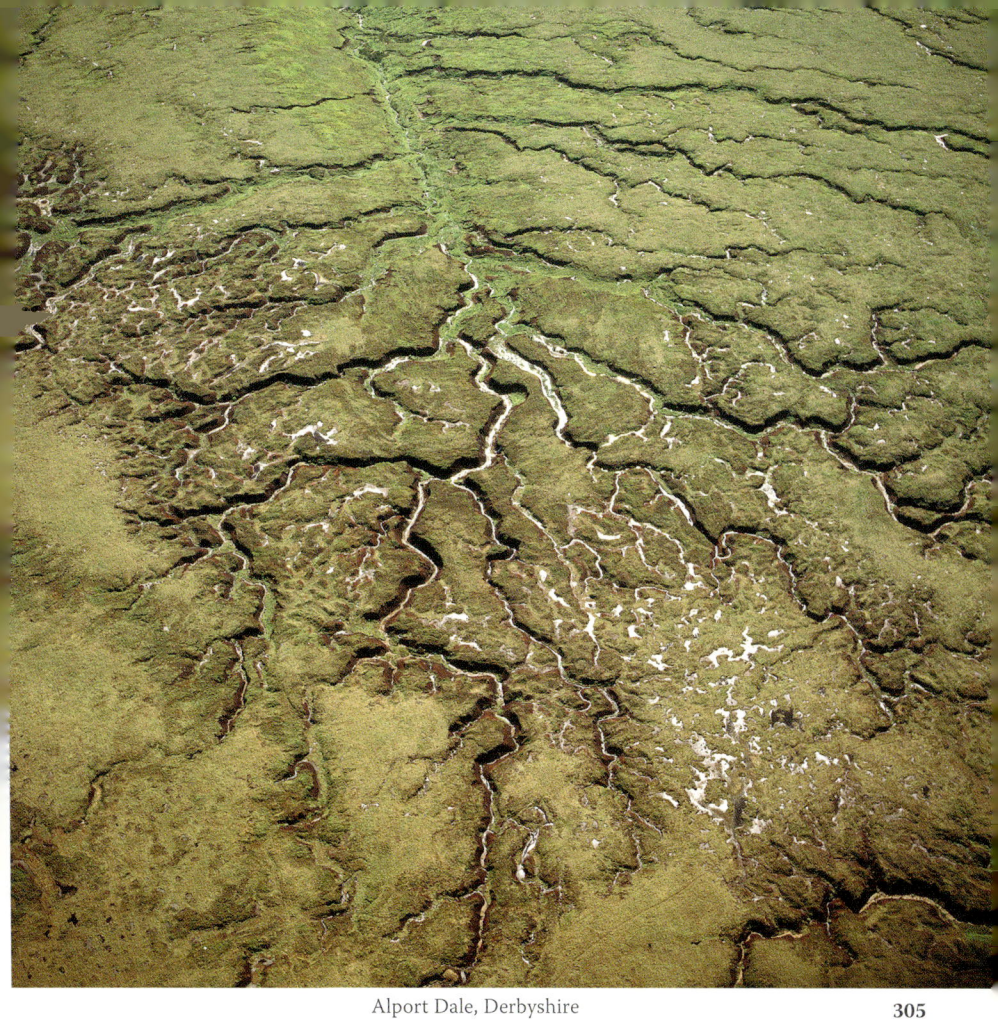

Alport Dale, Derbyshire

Abney Low, Abney, Derbyshire

Mam Tor, Derbyshire

Arbor Low Stone Circle, Derbyshire

Welbeck Abbey, Nottinghamshire

Sherwood Forest and River Poulter, Nottinghamshire

Frampton Marsh, The Wash, Lincolnshire

Burghley House, Lincolnshire

Lincoln Cathedral, Lincolnshire

Ingleborough, North Yorkshire

IX: YORKSHIRE

Yorkshire borders the North Sea from the Humber Estuary north to Cleveland, and stretches westwards all the way to Cumbria, Lancashire and Greater Manchester. It is England's largest county, so big in fact that it used to be divided into North, East and West "Ridings", a legacy from the Vikings who settled here in the ninth century. In 1974, many English counties were reorganised and Yorkshire was divided into four parts: North, South, East and West. York is the regional capital, which in Roman times, was second only in importance to London. Yorkshire today is a beautiful county with open moors, dales, and mountainous landscapes divided by valleys of rich meadows, with ancient villages and industrial towns. The North Sea coast at Flamborough Head is spectacular, with cliffs that provide nesting ledges for seabirds, among them gannets, which have reached record numbers at the Bempton Cliffs Nature Reserve. Further north is the Victorian resort town of Scarborough, and Whitby, home to one of England's oldest abbeys. To the south, the long coastline of Bridlington Bay is continually eroding. Houses, even whole villages, now lie submerged beneath the sea. Further south is the Humber Estuary and the impressive Humber suspension bridge, linking Yorkshire to Lincolnshire.

Natural resources have been mined in Yorkshire for centuries. Its coal seams are on the edge of the greatest region of coalfields in Britain. Iron ore has been smelted in Sheffield using charcoal since before the fourteenth century and steel products, for which the town is famous, followed the invention of the crucible process in 1740, expanding when the Bessemer process introduced stainless steel in the nineteenth century. The twentieth century saw the expansion of industry, road systems and communication networks on an unprecedented scale, so the landscape bears little resemblance to how it looked when early neolithic hunters first set foot here. Then, it was wild and remote, with plenty of game, and caves in which to shelter. For the pastoralists who settled around 3000 BC, it was ideal country for sheep. A wealth of earthworks, barrows, cairns, stone circles and hill forts lie scattered across the landscape as a reminder of times past. A cluster of three ancient interconnecting henges at Thornborough, North Yorkshire, is of international importance, comparable to those at Stonehenge and Avebury. The only other similar henge complex known in England is at Priddy, on the Mendip Hills in Somerset, where there are four circles, though not so clearly defined. The Thornborough henges formed an important centre for ritual ceremonies between 4000 and 2000 BC. Each of the circles is massive, with a maximum diameter of about 244 metres (800 feet): the northernmost is well preserved, but the other two have been damaged by repeated ploughing. The future survival of all three is now threatened by encroaching gravel quarries. Occasionally, excavations for building schemes uncover secrets from the past. In West Yorkshire, the construction of a new motorway unearthed an Iron Age Celtic chariot, together with the skeleton of an adult male. Only nineteen other chariot burials were previously known in Britain, nearly all of them in East Yorkshire, around Wetwang. Dating from 500-100 BC, they are the burials of elite individuals, often accompanied by high status objects. Celtic chariot burials are unusual, set in square-shaped barrows similar to those found in the Champagne-Ardennes region of France, and the Mosel region of Germany. It is possible that some form of association existed between the people in these areas. The Celts traveled widely, not only for trade but also for settlement, and there may have been kinship links with the folk who settled in Yorkshire.

Some 330 million years ago, Yorkshire was a shallow tropical sea and the layers of sediment that accumulated on the seabed eventually compacted into limestone. Later, Ice Age glaciers scraped the limestone clean in places, exposing it to centuries of rain, which ate into the surface forming runnels and fractures. The resulting geological formations are spectacular, and examples can be seen in the Yorkshire Dales on Ingleborough and above Malham. Malham Cove is a huge limestone cliff, once the site of an 80 metres (260 feet) high waterfall. The waterfall is now dry, the river having found an alternative subterranean route, emerging at the foot of the cliff as a small stream called Malham Beck. Underground, throughout the area, streams have created honeycombs of countless caverns and tunnels, in places a wonderland of stalactites and stalagmites up to 350 million years old. Between Swaledale and Wensleydale, sited by a high mountain road leading across the moors, there is a line of fluted limestone potholes famously known as the "Buttertubs". Tradition has it that, long ago, farmers would suspend their butter and cheese in sacks overnight in the deep, cool fissures here before resuming their long journeys to market.

The beautiful Yorkshire Dales stretch from the heights of the Pennines, at well over 700 metres (2,300 feet), down a series of beautiful valleys towards the Vale of York. Many of the Dales have familiar names, such as Wensleydale, famous for its cheese, and Swaledale, with its ancient fields of luxuriant green grass divided by stone walls. The valley flanks can be steep and rocky, levelling out on to high moorland covered by heather and bracken. Dominating the area are the three peaks of Whernside, Ingleborough and Pen-y-Ghent. The Pennine Way long distance footpath passes over the top of Pen-y-Ghent at 693 metres (2,273 feet).

Wind and moving glaciers sculpted the exposed Brimham Rocks, near Pateley Bridge, into fantastic shapes that drew the attention of neolithic and Bronze Age peoples, who carved hundreds of petroglyphs there. Rock carvings have been discovered elsewhere too, on the moors south of Ilkley, around Fylingdales, and on Askwith Moor, where there is a petroglyph depicting a human figure. On the steep hillside of Roulston Scar, overlooking the Vale of York, is another carved symbol. It is not a prehistoric rock carving, nor is it an Iron Age hill figure, although it looks like one. The Kilburn White Horse was created, in 1857, by Thomas Taylor, who was influenced by the famous Wiltshire horse hill figures. At 97 metres (318 feet) long, it is the most northerly and one of England's largest hill figures.

Before the Roman invasion of Britain, the area that is now northern England was controlled by a confederation of Celtic tribes known as the Brigantes. In AD 71, the Roman governor of Britain, Quintus Petillius Cerialis, sent the 9th Roman legion to try to subdue the tribes, but instead they faced unrelenting rebellion. The Romans built a fort between the River Foss and the River Ouse where York now stands, and they called the town that grew up around it *Eboracum*. Strong protective walls were built, forming the base of the city walls that remain today. So important did York become in Roman Britain that a royal palace was built in the city, and the Emperor Septimius Severus stayed there with his imperial court until AD 211. The military importance of York was so strong that it remained an army base until 2000, when the government decided to close the army headquarters there, thus severing nearly two millennia of military history and tradition. Although some of the historic city's walls and gates were demolished in the early nineteenth century, there are still some Roman remains in York today, including a ten-sided tower and a few sections of the original walls. Hidden beneath the city, Roman sewers still run. The majority of the existing city wall dates from the twelfth to the fourteenth century. The rectangular gatehouse of Micklegate Bar marks the main entrance to the city, and was the place where traitor's heads were displayed, following executions, as a deterrent to rebellion.

The Romans abandoned *Eboracum* around AD 407, and the city fell into decay, until the arrival of the Angles and the Saxons. Some Saxons originally came to Britain as mercenaries in the Roman army, but after the Romans left, the Saxons and their Germanic relatives the Angles and Jutes overcame the native Britons in a series of raids from across the North Sea. Under the Saxons the city of York was renamed *Eoferwic,* and became the capital of the Saxon kingdom of *Deirwa,* which extended from the Tees to the Humber. When, the Christian Princess Ethelburga of Kent came here in 627 to marry King Edwin of Northumbria, Edwin was baptised by Bishop Paulinus in a church specially constructed for the purpose at a holy well. The wooden building, of which nothing survives, was reputed to be the first York Minster. It was rebuilt in stone a few years later, and dedicated to St. Peter. York was to become an ecclesiastical centre second only to Canterbury in importance, and the seat of Britain's second archbishopric. The prosperity of Anglo-Saxon York in the ninth century made it an obvious target for Danish Vikings. An invasion force led by Ivar the Boneless captured the city, and changed its name to *Jorvik.* At about this time, Norwegian settlers from Ireland moved eastwards across the Pennines into the Dales from Cumbria, bringing with them their skills of pastoral farming. Many of the local names for landscape features such as beck, clint, crag, fell, gill, mere, moss, rigg, scar and tarn are derived from Norse words. The Viking influence in York lasted less than a century; in 954, Eric Bloodaxe was defeated by King Eadred of Wessex. However, local rebellions and repeated invasions from Norway kept the north of England in a state of turmoil.

When Edward the Confessor died in January 1066, his brother-in-law Harold became king despite reputedly having sworn to Edward's cousin, Duke William of Normandy, that he would not claim the throne. William determined to take it by force, and while he waited for a month for a good wind to carry his army across the Channel, King Harold Hardrada of Norway brought another invasion force across the North Sea, sailing up the Humber and the Ouse to take York. On 25th September, the Norse king went to Stamford Bridge, just 13 kilometres (8 miles) from York, to talk to local leaders, but was taken by surprise by the English army, and defeated. Meanwhile, William's invasion force finally crossed the Channel, so Harold and his army headed south as fast as they could. The famous Battle of Hastings, a major turning point in English history, took place three weeks later. It left Harold dead, and England in the hands of the Normans. The northern part of England rebelled against the Norman forces, who retaliated so brutally with fire and sword that there was little left. They burned villages, slaughtered people and their livestock, and left the corpses to rot where they fell. The Domesday Book survey of 1086 records the north as a wasteland.

It took generations for the area to recover. Meanwhile, before 1216, Norman barons built 22 castles in Yorkshire, the Minster at York and the Minster at Beverley, churches, abbeys, and monasteries. By the time of the Dissolution of the Monasteries by King Henry VIII, there were more monasteries in Yorkshire than any other county in England. The magnificent ruin of Fountains Abbey still provides a glimpse of its awe inspiring former grandeur and bears testament to the skill of the masons. The long, vaulted cellarium, over 90 metres (nearly 300 feet) long, survives little altered since its construction, its ribbed vault supported by nineteen central pillars. The Romans, the Saxons, and the Normans all left their influences on the Yorkshire landscape. The Romans built roads; the Saxons shaped the countryside with fields and villages that, for the most part, still exist today; and the Normans left us their architecture in castles, cathedrals and churches. All this came at a huge cost in blood and suffering, and perhaps explains the famous resilience and survival instinct of the people from this part of England.

Pen-y-Ghent, North Yorkshire

Buttertubs Pass, North Yorkshire

Grimwith Reservoir, North Yorkshire

Gouthwaite Reservoir, North Yorkshire

Angram Reservoir, North Yorkshire

Scar House Reservoir, North Yorkshire

Semer Water, North Yorkshire

Malham Tarn, North Yorkshire

River Ure, near Middleham, North Yorkshire

Addlebrough, North Yorkshire

Malham, North Yorkshire

Malham Cove, North Yorkshire

Swaledale near Crackpot, North Yorkshire

Muker, North Yorkshire

Ribblehead Viaduct, Settle-Carlisle Railway, North Yorkshire

Arten Gill Viaduct, Settle-Carlisle Railway, North Yorkshire

Brimham Rocks, North Yorkshire

Thornborough Circles, North Yorkshire

Studley Royal Water Garden, North Yorkshire

Fountains Abbey, North Yorkshire

Jervaulx Abbey, North Yorkshire

Bolton Priory, North Yorkshire

Richmond Castle, North Yorkshire

Middleham Castle, North Yorkshire

Easby Abbey, North Yorkshire

Rievaulx Abbey, North Yorkshire

Byland Abbey, North Yorkshire

Roche Abbey, South Yorkshire

Castle Bolton, North Yorkshire

Conisbrough Castle, South Yorkshire

347

Castle Howard, North Yorkshire

Helmsley Castle, North Yorkshire

Helperby, North Yorkshire

North Yorkshire Moors, North Yorkshire

Beverley Minster, East Yorkshire (Humberside)

York Minster, North Yorkshire

Flamborough Head, North Yorkshire

Bempton Cliffs, North Yorkshire

Scarborough Castle, North Yorkshire

Whitby Abbey, North Yorkshire

Kilburn White Horse, North Yorkshire

Humber Bridge, East Yorkshire

Stone Walls at Wasdale Head, Cumbria

X: THE NORTH WEST

Cheshire, Cumbria, Greater Manchester, Lancashire, Merseyside

The famous Lake District of Cumbria, one of the most picturesque and spectacular areas of England, which was established as a National Park in 1951, nestles in the North West. Here are the principal English lakes, set in luxuriant valleys and surrounded by mountains, of which Scafell Pike, at 978 metres (3,210 feet) is the highest in England, commanding an awe inspiring view over Wast Water, the deepest lake. Not far away, Windermere is the largest and best-known lake. The valleys, with their lakes, radiate from a central core of hump-backed mountains, composed of some of the world's oldest rock formations, formed some 500 million years ago and eroded by glacial action that created hanging valleys with attractive waterfalls and remote tarns. The richness of the landscape is impressive; the poet William Wordsworth (1770-1850) became so inspired by this place that in his Guide to the Lakes, published in 1820, he wrote: *'I do not indeed know any tract of country in which, within so narrow a compass, may be found an equal variety in the influences of light and shadow, upon the sublime or beautiful features of landscape'.*

Cumbria is also famous for its ancient stone circles. Around five thousand years ago, groups of people started to create circles of huge stones, arranging them so that the alignment of each matched the seasonal movements of the sun, moon, and certain stars. There are some fifty neolithic and Bronze Age stone circles in Cumbria, including some of the earliest known in Britain. We gaze in awe at these monuments, both for their age and for the genius in their design. Castlerigg Stone Circle, near Keswick, is 30 metres (about 100 feet) in diameter and is one of the most visually impressive. The 38 stones, some standing over 1.5 metres (5 feet) in height, are on the crest of a low hill with views across to Skiddaw, Blencathra and Lonscale Fell. Another stone circle, one of the finest in the north of England and the second biggest in the country, is Long Meg and her 'daughters', near Penrith. It dates from about 1500 BC, and has a diameter of over 100 metres (328 feet). 'Long Meg' is the tallest of the 69 stones, at 3.5 metres (about 12 feet) high, and stands a short distance outside the circle. Its four corners face the points of the compass, and it is engraved with mysterious symbols. These sites were meeting places and were used for religious rituals. Together with the communities who built them, and the trails that linked one with another, the circles formed a network for communication and for trade in stone axes and other goods. At Langdale Pikes, in the central fells of the Lake District, slate axes were quarried for trade all over Europe.

Few stone circles can have such an incongruous setting as that at Grey Croft. A few hundred metres north of the ten ancient stones is Sellafield Nuclear Site, on the coast of the Irish Sea, the world's first commercial nuclear power station, which has operated since the early 1950's. Currently, there are two types of nuclear installations there, one to provide electricity for the national grid, and the Windscale Nuclear Reactor, producing plutonium for defence. There is also a reprocessing plant, where spent fuel from nuclear reactors worldwide is converted into re-useable uranium and plutonium. It also processes radioactive waste - a daunting undertaking.

The task of finding sustainable and safe sources of energy has led to the construction of wind turbines. Exposed to the prevailing weather from the Atlantic Ocean, Britain is ideally placed for harnessing the wind to produce clean electricity without the greenhouse gas penalty paid by conventional power stations. There are snags however. Although efficiency is improving, wind turbines only produce relatively small amounts of electricity, so thousands of them are required to achieve the sort of output that will match our present rate of consumption. Furthermore, because the wind does not blow all the time, conventional power stations are still required as 'back-up'. The turbines, with their huge whirling blades, are usually constructed on exposed and open countryside, but with a height up to that of a 30-storey high-rise building, wind farms can be seen for miles. Pylons and transmission lines are then required to carry the power to the national grid, increasing the impact on the landscape. At the time of writing, there are ten operational wind farms in Cumbria, and this number is set to grow.

Some of the most important industrial areas in the country are located at Merseyside and Greater Manchester; in fact, significant developments of the Industrial Revolution began around the Mersey, bringing both prosperity and poverty, as well as pollution. Liverpool began as a fishing village in the thirteenth century, but grew rapidly during the eighteenth century in line with industrial development. It once claimed to be Europe's greatest Atlantic seaport, with 11 kilometres (7 miles) of docks and the world's largest floating landing stage. Apart from industry, it is famous culturally, flourishing in its musical and artistic traditions. Liverpool has two cathedrals, of which the Anglican cathedral, finished in red sandstone and completed in 1978, is huge and second in size only to St. Peter's in Rome. Across the Mersey from Liverpool, a Benedictine Priory was founded at Birkenhead in the twelfth century. At that time, it was a secluded spot screened by forests. Even in the nineteenth century, Birkenhead was a quiet hamlet, then, in 1817, a steam ferry to cross the Mersey to Liverpool began operating, opening the area up to settlers. The first docks opened in 1847, and this, together with shipbuilding, became major influences on the development of the area.

Around Wigan, in Greater Manchester, coal has been mined for centuries, but the last mine in the area closed in 1992. In the nineteenth century, Wigan became known as "Coalopolis"- the 'capital' for coal, helping the development of the textile industries at centres such as Burnley and Bury. John Kay invented the Flying Shuttle in Bury, making looms more efficient. In Blackburn, in 1760, James Hargreaves invented a carding machine that ranged cotton fibres, removing unripe seeds and other impurities. In 1764, he also invented the Spinning Jenny, and in 1769, Richard Arkwright, from Preston, invented the Spinning Frame. The Industrial Revolution was a time for great innovation, but the introduction of machinery that reduced the need for manual labour brought social problems. People from the countryside were still swarming into the towns and cities seeking a better life only to find appalling squalor, disease, moral degradation and poverty. It resulted in riots and the destruction of machinery by the Luddites in the 1820s, in protest that their livelihoods were threatened.

As soon as the Industrial Revolution gathered momentum, an efficient way to transport goods between mines, factories and ports was desperately needed. Roads were inadequate, so a network of canals was built by groups of workers known as "navvies", who came from all over the country as well as from Ireland. The Weaver Navigation scheme provided an outlet to the Mersey for Cheshire salt; the Sankey and Bridgewater Canals served the Lancashire coalfields; and the Manchester Ship Canal, which finally opened in 1894, made Manchester an inland port. The navvies went on to build the railways; back-breaking work, using picks and shovels to lay out thousands of miles of rail lines without the aid of any machinery. The new railways not only made a huge impact on the emerging industrial nation but also made traveling much easier, leading to the growth of seaside resorts. Southport still retains some of its Victorian elegance, while Blackpool has grown into a sort of British Las Vegas, its shoreline bristling with amusement arcades, casinos, bingo halls and a 158 metres (518 feet) high tower - its prominent landmark. Further north is Morecambe Bay, Britain's largest continuous area of inter-tidal mud flats and sand bars, and England's second largest bay after the Wash. The marine habitats range from fringing salt marsh and huge areas of sand and tidal mud flats, to dense beds of mussels and cockles, which can cover the surface of every available boulder. It also provides a refuge for birds, including pink-footed geese, shelduck, grey plover, knot, dunlin, bar-tailed godwit, and breeding populations of sandwich terns.

One of the treasures of the North West is the city of Chester, in Cheshire, rich in archaeological remains from the time of the Roman occupation. Its harbour and strategic position made it an important outpost of the Roman Empire, and in AD 70, it was the fortress of the 20th legion, the *Valeria Victrix*. The Romans controlled the entire North West; at that time, the people of Wales and Cumbria were known collectively as *Cymry*, the Celtic word for "compatriots". At the beginning of the seventh century, the Anglian empire expanded, and the majority of Cumbria came under their control following a battle at Chester in 615. The Normans reached Chester in 1070 and built Chester Castle. Soon the city became affluent once again, until the fifteenth century when silt from the River Dee gradually disabled it as a port. Over the centuries, the Roman walls have remained virtually intact, and the city also has many distinctive medieval features, including the famous multi-storeyed 'Rows', whose layout dates from the thirteenth century.

By the early tenth century, much of Cumbria was under the control of the English King Edmund I, who gave it to the Scots King Malcolm I in return for support in defending the north against the Vikings. From that time, until the eighteenth century, the ownership of Carlisle and Cumbria was continually fought over, and changed hands many times between the Scots and the English. The reign of Edward I, King of England (1272-1307), was dominated by constant wars with Scotland. In 1297, the Scots army, led by William Wallace and Andrew de Moray, resisted English brutality by taking Stirling Castle, followed by violent cross border incursions in Cumbria and Northumberland. Farms and churches in the Lake District were destroyed, abbeys plundered and burned, people and cattle were slaughtered. For protection, the wealthy people of Cumbria and Northumberland built defensive structures known as pele towers, stone buildings usually of three storeys, with walls up to 3 metres (10 feet) thick, designed to withstand short sieges.

Today Carlisle, close to the border of Scotland, is the capital of Cumbria. In AD 78, the Roman Governor Agricola built a wooden fort on the site where the castle now stands, and gave it the name *Luguvalium*. From there, the Romans tried to defeat the Caledonian tribes but it proved to be a difficult task. The Emperor Hadrian therefore ordered the construction of a defensive wall to mark the northern limit of his empire across the neck of England from Wallsend, on the River Tyne in the east, to Bowness-on-Solway in the west. Beginning in AD 122, it took some four years, at a huge cost in men and resources. Sixteen forts were built along its length and between these were placed mile castles and turrets. The strategic position of the wall was critical, so the course chosen followed the crest of ridges formed by the volcanic Whin Sill with very steep flanks facing north, adding to the effectiveness of the barrier. It was 117 kilometres (73 miles) long, and cut right through territory held by the Brigantes, so for a while at least the Romans must have faced skirmishes with the tribe on both sides. Hadrian's Wall invokes a dramatic image of a country divided by conflict and occupation. After nearly 2,000 years, it still looks impressive, its sinuous course tracing the contours of the wild landscape of northern England from horizon to horizon. As a boundary, it must have been formidable. With its aid, the Romans struggled to control this remote corner of their Empire for 300 years.

Stainton Fell, Lake District, Cumbria

Wast Water, Lake District, Cumbria

Derwent Water, Lake District, Cumbria

Derwent Water and Keswick, Lake District, Cumbria

Derwent Fell, Lake Distict, Cumbria

Coniston and Coniston Water, Lake District, Cumbria

Ambleside and Lake Windermere, Lake District, Cumbria

Bowness-on-Windermere, Lake District, Cumbria

Haweswater, Lake District, Cumbria

Ullswater, Lake District, Cumbria

Scafell Pike, Lake District, Cumbria

Valley north of Lake Thirlmere, Lake District, Cumbria

Castlerigg Stone Circle, Cumbria

Castlerigg Stone Circle, Cumbria

Dacre Castle, Cumbria

N 54°38′00″ W 002°50′10″

Greystoke Castle, Cumbria

Hadrian's Wall, looking west from Housesteads Roman Fort

Wetheral, Cumbria

Solway Firth, Cumbria

The River Eden flowing into the Solway Firth, Cumbria

Piel Castle and Piel Island, Cumbria

Barrow-in-Furness, Cumbria

Wind Farm at Kirkby Moor, Cumbria

Blackpool, Lancashire

Mud Flats on the River Lune, near Lancaster, Lancashire

Lancaster Castle, Lancashire

Liverpool Anglican Cathedral, Merseyside

Liverpool Waterfront, Merseyside

N 53º 07' 08", W 0.00 m m [unclear]

Little Moreton Hall, Cheshire

Chester, Cheshire

Beeston Castle, Cheshire

Peckforton Castle, Cheshire

Holmes Chapel Viaduct, Cheshire

Jodrell Bank, Cheshire

Housesteads Roman Fort and Hadrian's Wall, Northumberland

XI: THE NORTH EAST

Cleveland, Durham, Northumberland, Tyne and Wear

The North East of England was, for centuries, a bloody arena, firstly for unending squabbles and skirmishes between the Scots and the English, and also resistance against the Norman invasion for which the people paid a heavy price. William the Conqueror's men adopted a scorched earth policy, leaving total devastation in their wake. The border troubles continued for hundreds of years. By the sixteenth century, over a hundred castles, plus many smaller fortified houses with peles or bastles, existed here, a testimony to the insecurity of the region, and Berwick-upon-Tweed, now the most northerly town in England, has changed hands between England and Scotland thirteen times. Until the reign of King James I in the early seventeenth century, and the Act of Union between England and Scotland in 1707, life in the border country was one of strife and misery, and peace did not arrive overnight. Gradually, though, Northumberland was transformed into peaceful farm country, but even today, this frontier land holds a sparse population unmatched anywhere else in England, and a sense of quiet remoteness pervades the landscape.

Before the time of the Romans, the whole region was the haunt of warring tribes and the building of Hadrian's Wall, the most important surviving monument left by the Romans in Britain, was an attempt to control them. As a feat of engineering, the wall was remarkable, 6 metres (20 feet) high, 3 metres (10 feet) wide and built of stone from coast to coast. Its defences were supplemented by a military road for patrols and supplies, and an earthwork called a *vallum*, which formed a boundary on the southern side. Within this military zone were 16 forts of which the surviving ruin of Housesteads is a fine example. Along the wall itself were mile castles and in between these were turrets. The 12,000 men employed on this defensive barrier came not necessarily from Italy, but from all parts of the Roman Empire, as far away as North Africa, Iraq and Syria.

Housesteads fort is close to the halfway point along the wall, just inside Northumberland. Its perimeter wall is still intact, and inside are the ruins of several buildings, including the commander's house, granaries, barrack blocks and communal latrines. When forts like this were active, communities grew around them, with skilled craftsmen, traders and their families, a supporting infrastructure for soldiers working in a remote place, and native Britons intermarried with Roman soldiers of many different nationalities. From the middle of the third century, the Roman Empire came increasingly under threat on the continent, and the need for reinforcements there depleted the size of the Roman garrison stationed in Britain. By AD 367, the number of soldiers defending Hadrian's Wall had reached an all time low, and Pictish tribes overran it several times on raids. Rome's hold on this northern frontier became increasingly untenable, and before the end of the fourth century, the Empire was crumbling. A full-scale evacuation of troops from Britain began, and soon afterwards, the Roman occupation was over. The Romans had defended northern Britain from attacks by the Picts, but they had also built watchtowers along the coast to counter raids by Angle and Saxon invaders. As soon as the Roman forces withdrew, the raiders had a free rein in a Britain that was vulnerable and ripe for the taking. Angles began to settle along the east coast, claiming the region they called East Anglia by 440, together with Lincolnshire, and soon they advanced northwards to Yorkshire.

The Kingdom of Northumbria was established by the Anglo-Saxon King Aethelfrith, who ruled from 592-616. When he was killed in battle, his children fled to Scotland where they met Irish monks from Iona and converted to the Christian faith. The second son of Aethelfrith, Oswald, succeeded to the throne in 634. From Bamburgh, the site of his fortress on an outcrop of volcanic rock on the coast, he invited the monks of Iona to send a missionary. Aidan arrived in AD 635 and, together with 12 other monks, settled on an island called Lindisfarne off the coast between Berwick and Bamburgh. From there, they spread the holy message across the land. Aidan realised, however, that he needed to educate more people to become missionaries; otherwise, his efforts might die with him. So, Lindisfarne became one of the first educational institutions, teaching the skills of reading and writing in Latin.

The Farne Islands, a wildlife haven situated off the coast near Bamburgh, are home to 50,000 pairs of puffins, and a 4,000-strong colony of the rare grey seal, the largest carnivore in Britain. From AD 640, monks, who went there to find solitude and to meditate, periodically inhabited the Farnes. Aidan was the first, although it was St. Cuthbert who made the islands famous. He was prior at Lindisfarne, but retired to Inner Farne in 676, building himself a shelter from rocks and turf. The living conditions, especially in the winter, must have been severe, but he stayed alone there for eight years. When he died, he was buried at Lindisfarne, which flourished until 793, when Vikings from Norway raided the island. The monks who survived the attack fled, carrying with them the exhumed body of St Cuthbert to Durham, where the cathedral was founded as a shrine for him. After the Norman Conquest, Benedictine monks from Durham renamed Lindisfarne 'Holy Island' to commemorate the holy blood shed during the Viking raid. They built a new Priory on the island that remained until King Henry VIII's Dissolution of the Monasteries in 1536, when its stone was plundered to build Lindisfarne Castle, to defend the island against possible Scots' incursions. Just two of the many bloody battles that have been fought on Northumbrian soil between the Scots and the English were those at Otterburn, in 1388, and at Flodden, in 1513. At Otterburn, the Douglases of Scotland defeated the Percys of Northumberland, while at the Battle of Flodden the English defeated the Scots, for whom it was a disaster. The king, many of his countrymen, and prominent members of almost all the noble families of Scotland were killed that day.

The area of Northumberland around Flodden Field is very rich in Bronze Age rock carvings and Iron Age hill forts. Near Doddington can be found the Dod Law Iron Age forts, together with many Bronze Age rock carvings. 3 kilometres (2 miles) to the east of Ford, the Roughting Linn rock carving is the largest in England, a spectacular expanse of sandstone, 18 metres (59 feet) long, decorated with over sixty carvings. On one of the more prominent of the Cheviot Hills is Yeavering Bell, on which was sited the largest known Iron Age hill fort in Northumberland. A surrounding stone wall encloses 5.3 hectares (13 acres) and there are traces of at least 130 huts. Further south, at Ingram, are the Greaves Ash hut circles and enclosure. This is the largest known group of Iron Age stone hut circles, about forty of them, each 6 metres (20 feet) across, with paved floors.

Today, Northumberland's National Park covers a huge area of moorland and hill country with forested valleys, broken in the south by dales and green meadows, from the Cheviot Hills on the Scottish border, south to Hadrian's Wall. The upland heather moorland of the Cheviot Hills developed over thousands of years as ancient woodlands were cleared to introduce cattle and sheep. Deliberate burning of small areas at different times produces an interesting mosaic of young and old heather plants, to provide food, shelter and nesting areas for grouse, and tender young shoots for sheep. The rivers are home for otters, and fish like salmon and sea trout migrate from the sea upstream to lay their eggs. Bordering on to the National Park is Kielder Water, the largest man-made lake in Europe. The lake sits within the massive Kielder Forest, the largest in Britain. Predominantly a planted forest of Sitka and Norway spruce, it is currently being replanted to include a wider range of species, including many broadleaved trees. It is one of the last refuges for red squirrels, which cannot compete with the introduced grey squirrel, now common over most of Britain.

In contrast to the wilds of Northumberland is the industry in the south. Up in the fells of the Durham Pennines, where the dales and moors form a National Area of Outstanding Beauty, lead was mined from Roman times. The mature landscape of fields with hedgerows and dry stone walls, villages and market towns is also scarred by the old coalmines, and the steep contours of old slag heaps now covered with grass. Today, new scars are appearing, in the shape of huge, open cast coalmines and quarries. On the Tyne and Tees estuaries, there is heavy industry. In line with the Industrial Revolution of the seventeenth and eighteenth centuries, this area boomed. Today, Teesside is the site of one of the largest petrochemical industries in Europe, and is also a leading producer of iron and steel, so the deep-water ports of the River Tees are host to millions of tons of shipping each year. The abundance of natural resources stimulated the growth of industry. Coal was mined for centuries in the Tyne valley; during the reign of Queen Elizabeth I, demand for its use in London for cooking and heating grew rapidly, and, by 1640, coal from the Tyne valley supplied the nation, hence the familiar proverb 'coals to Newcastle'. The wealth generated brought prosperity, and the magnates of industry built fine houses, revitalized rural areas and local agriculture. The landscape designers laid out formal gardens and parks. Industrial development followed, and the world's earliest railways were developed here. By-products from coal mining were used in the production of glass and soap. Iron ore provided the lifeblood for the giant industries of shipbuilding, locomotive engineering, civil engineering and armaments manufacture. Newcastle upon Tyne began as a fort on Hadrian's Wall perched on the northern banks of the River Tyne, but today it is the cultural and industrial capital of the region. Its famous bridges include one of the first large-scale cast-iron bridges ever built. Gateshead is Newcastle's twin town, lying on the southern bank of the river. The uniquely design Gateshead Millennium Bridge, completed in 2001, was the first opening bridge to be built across the river for more than 100 years.

There are very few places left in England where it is possible to find a genuine unspoiled landscape, which looks as it might have done when neolithic peoples first roamed here. In a country as small as England, with such an intense history of invasion and occupation, of cosmopolitan culture, and of pioneering in industry, this is hardly surprising. Our great forests have been almost obliterated, to be exchanged for the familiar green patchwork of fields. Rivers have been tamed to create reservoirs and canals; the earth has been torn apart to yield its natural resources to feed industry, to build roads and railways, houses, towns, and cities. There are, perhaps, just a few last refuges on Dartmoor, in the Peak District, the Lake District, and the border country of Northumberland where moorland and mountain ridges can feel free of human influence. These are precious, isolated places where, even now, it is possible to walk unhindered by the noise of traffic, the orange glow in the sky from city lights at night, lines of pylons, and other scars of human interference. Here, with a little imagination, the land appears pristine and the only company is the gentle burble of a stream, the cry of a skylark and the touch of the wind.

Chesters Roman Fort, Hadrian's Wall, Northumberland

Corstopitum, Corbridge, Northumberland

Bamburgh Castle, Northumberland

Lindisfarne Castle, Lindisfarne or Holy Island, Northumberland

Lindisfarne Priory, Lindisfarne or Holy Island, Northumberland

Farne Islands, Northumberland

Berwick-upon-Tweed, Northumberland

Dunstanburgh Castle, Northumberland

Hulne Priory, Northumberland

Alnwick Castle, Northumberland

Warkworth Castle, Northumberland

Chillingham Castle, Northumberland

Poppy Field near Corbridge, Northumberland

Otterburn, Northumberland

Kielder Water & Kielder Forest, Northumberland

Northumberland National Park, Northumberland

St Mary's Island, Whitley Bay, Tyne & Wear

Tynemouth Priory and Castle, Tyne & Wear

Newcastle-upon-Tyne, Tyne & Wear

Gateshead Millennium Bridge, Tyne & Wear

Barnard Castle, Durham

Finchale Priory, Durham

Durham Cathedral, Durham

N 54° 46' 34" W 001° 34' 8"   Map Ref: 17 D1 18 I12

Raby Castle, Durham

Seal Sands, near Tees Estuary, Cleveland

Steel Works, Tees Estuary, Cleveland

Hartlepool, Cleveland

Redcar, Cleveland

List of photographs with page numbers and map references

ENGLAND

England is the largest of the countries comprising Great Britain, at 130,439 square kilometres (50,363 square miles) covering about two-thirds of the island, the remainder being shared by Scotland and Wales. As a country, it is smaller than the American State of Louisiana, or just over a quarter of the size of France with nearly the same population. England is part of the United Kingdom, which also includes Northern Ireland and a number of offshore islands. It is bounded on the north by Scotland; on the east by the North Sea; on the south by the English Channel; and on the west by the Atlantic Ocean, Wales, and the Irish Sea. Much of the country is gentle and low lying – the highest peak in England is Scafell Pike, at 978 metres (3,208 feet), in the beautiful Cumbrian mountains of the north west, where there are also several other peaks of similar height. Cumbria is the most rugged region in England and is more commonly known as the Lake District after the many lakes there. England's best-known river is the Thames, which rises in the Cotswold Hills in Gloucestershire to flow eastwards, eventually through London. The Thames is also England's longest river, at 346 kilometres (215 miles) in length. Actually, the River Severn is officially the longest in total, but its source and upper reaches are in the mountains of Wales making the section that runs through England shorter than the Thames. Although much of England was once covered by deciduous forest, today less than one per cent of it remains. The lowlands are dominated by meadows and pasture, with most industry located in the Midlands. Of the offshore islands, the Isle of Man and the Isle of Wight are the largest. The weather is temperate, kept mild and moist by the warm Atlantic Gulf Stream, with up to 1,000 mm (40 inches) of rain per year. The abundance of wet weather maintains our famous green landscape.

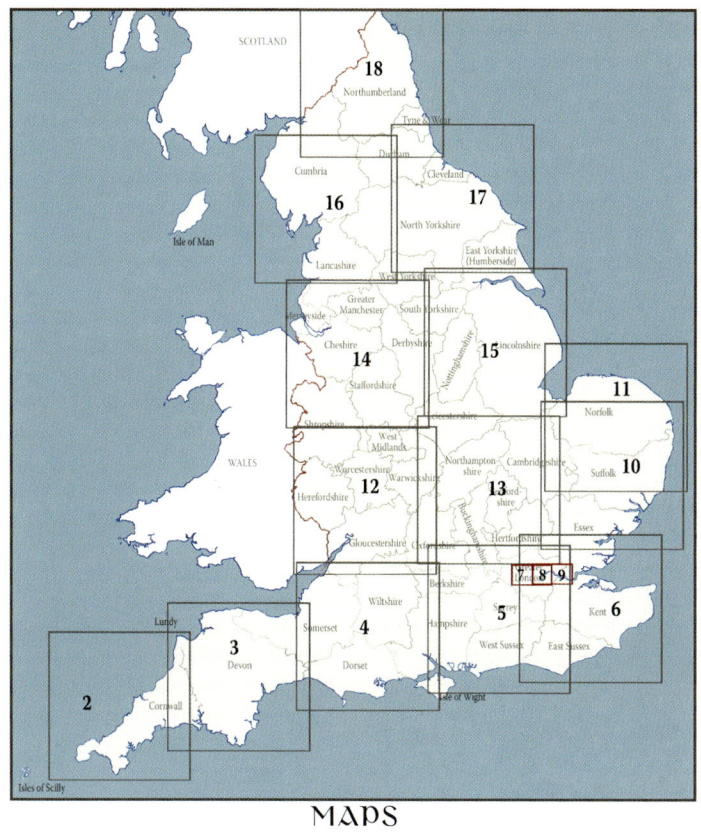

MAPS

══M1══ Motorway	══A3══	Primary Route
══A510══ Main Road	■ *Location*	Picture Location

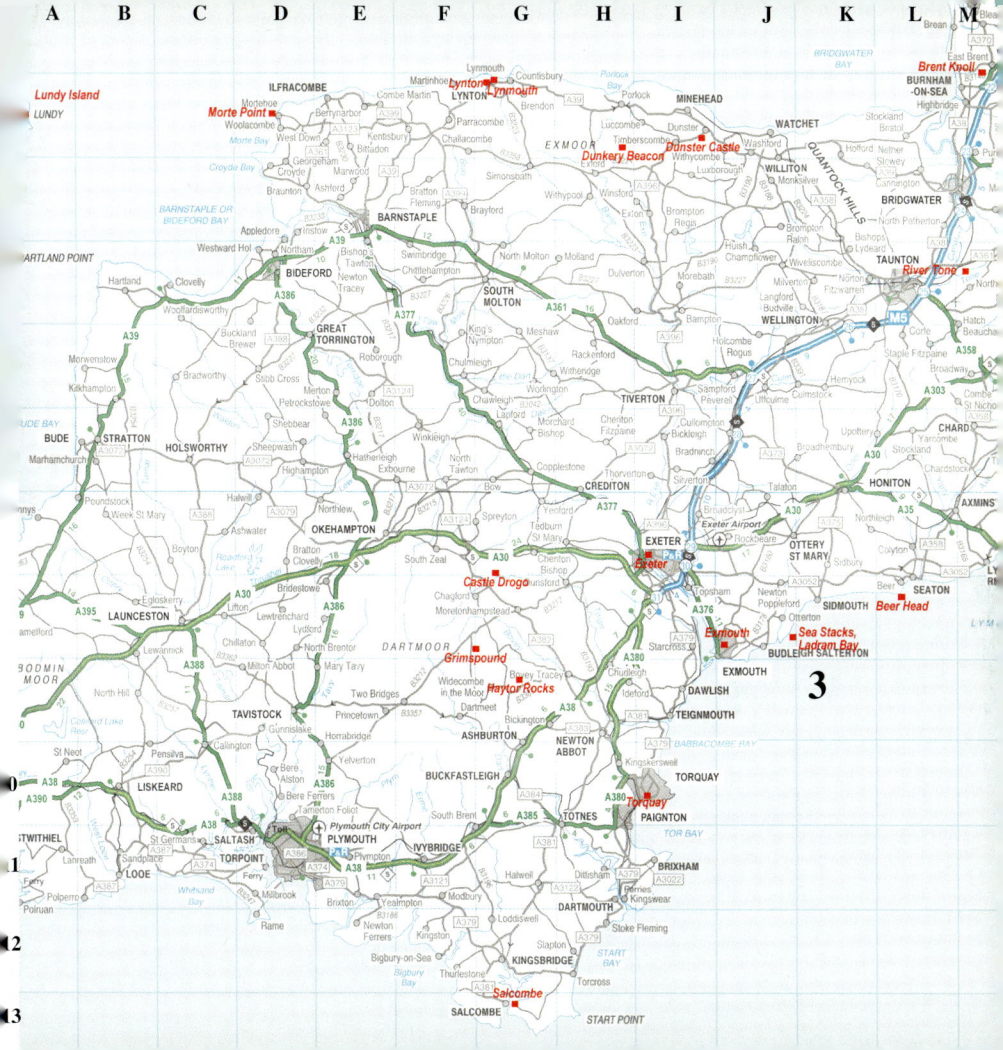

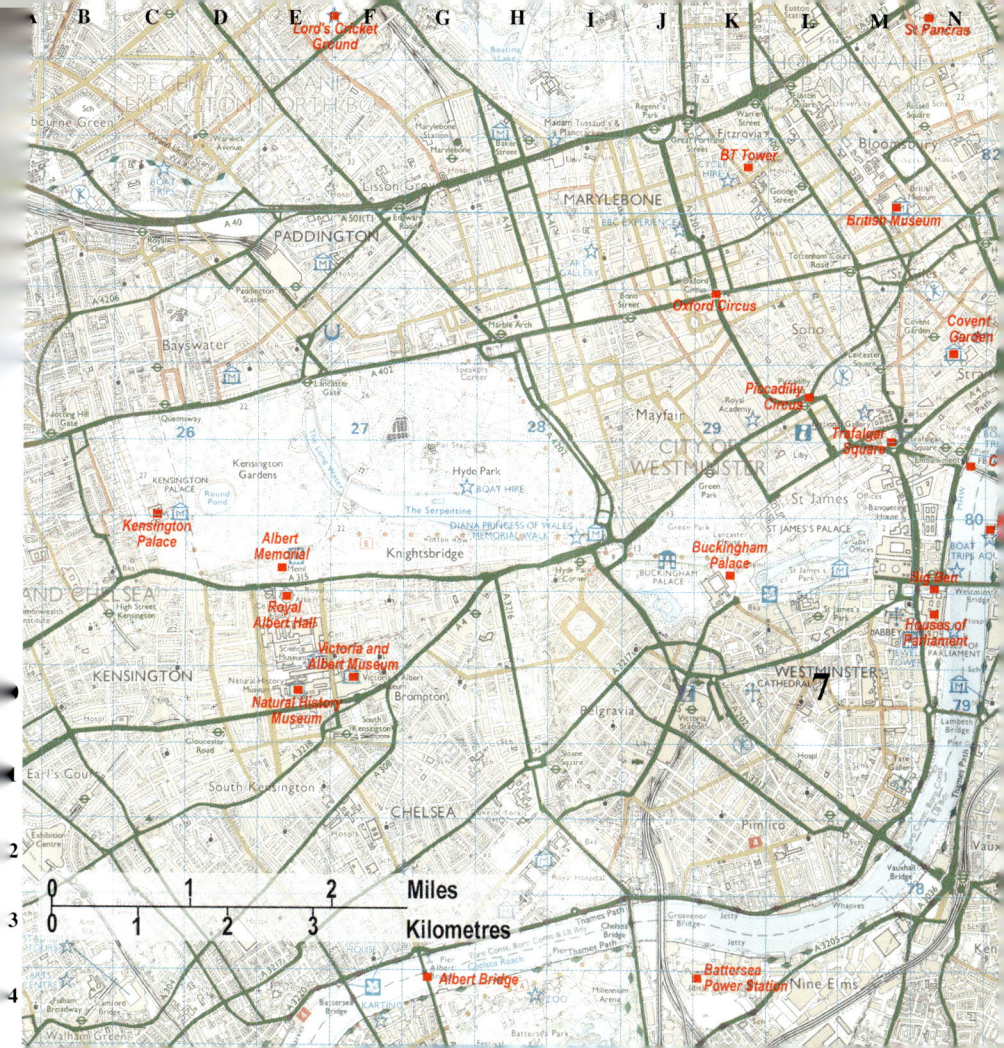

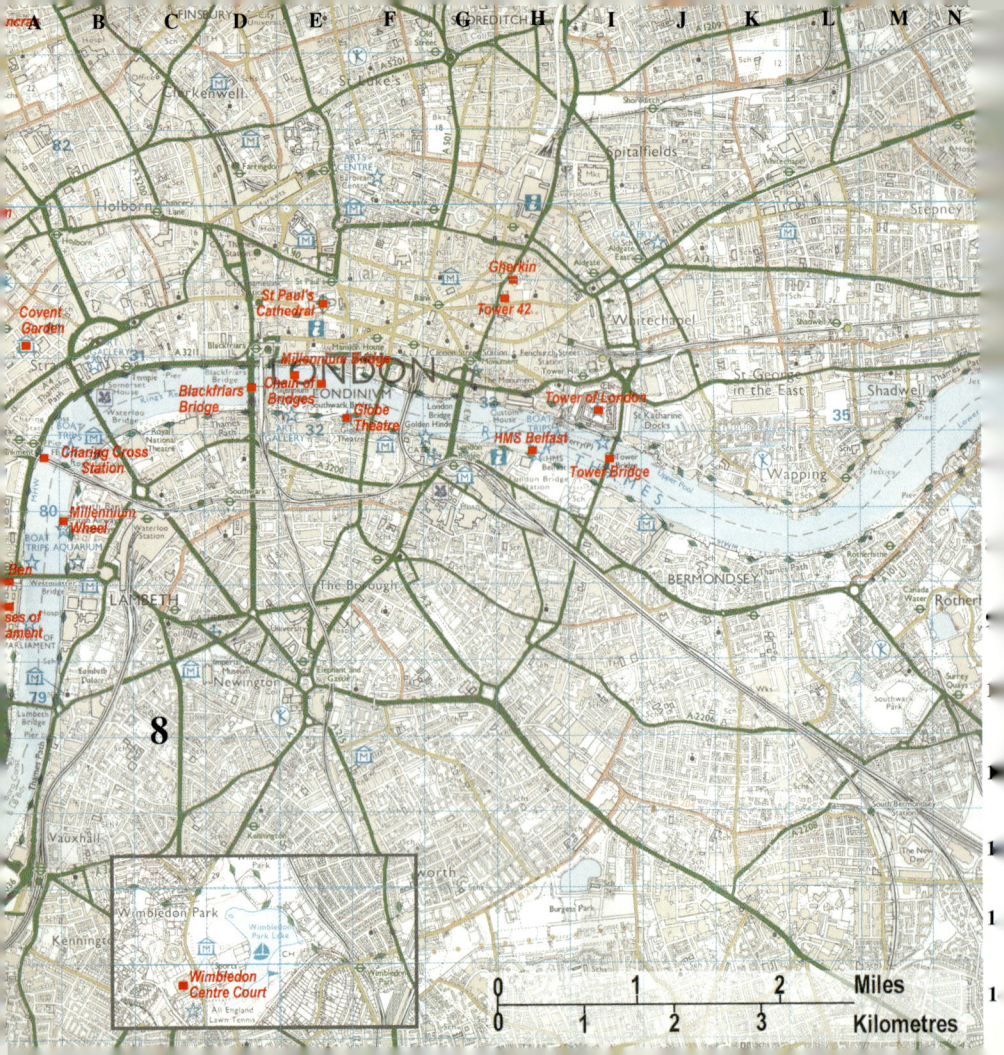

GREENWICH MERIDIAN

TOWER HAMLETS

Bromley

Plaistow

Limehouse

Bow Common

South Bromley

POPLAR   Blackwall

One Canada Square

Canary Wharf

Canning Town

Royal Victoria Dock

Exhibition Centre

Millennium Dome

Silvertown

The Thames Flood Barrier

Thames Barrier

ISLE OF DOGS

Cubitt Town

Millwall

Millwall Park

New Charlton

DEPTFORD

GREENWICH

GREENWICH AND WOOLWICH

Greenwich

Queen's House National Maritime Museum

37 38 39 40 41

81 80 79 9

Miles
0   1   2

Kilometres
0   1   2   3

INDEX

451

ACKNOWLEDGEMENTS

This book and its big sister *ENGLAND – An Aerial View* have been most enjoyable and interesting projects. Although primarily photographic works, the research gave us an excuse to read many books and papers written by eminent historians and archaeologists. Hundreds of books have been written on England's extraordinary history and the thought of adding yet more to the pile may not seem to be such a good idea, but what we have tried to do is to relate to our history through a simple appreciation of aerial photographs of the landscape. Even in books of this length, we knew we could not be comprehensive in either our photographic coverage or the text. We thought long and hard about what to include or leave out; inevitably, the choices were often difficult.

We would like to extend our thanks to the following people whose contributions made *ENGLAND – An Aerial View* possible: David Halford and Elizabeth Loving, who, together with Anne and Roger Martin, made invaluable suggestions with regard to the text; and Derek Sweet, who has kindly provided a home base for our aircraft.

As with any historical research, the preparation work revealed many records and writings that disagreed on dates or the course of events that happened a long time ago. Sometimes, the best one can hope for is to surmise the most likely version within the context of all the relevant information. We apologise most sincerely for any errors, or misrepresentations of facts or characters that we have inadvertently made.

ADRIAN WARREN has been making wildlife and environmental films for over thirty years, for the BBC, IMAX large format and National Geographic, and as an independent for his own company, Last Refuge Ltd. As a professional pilot, he specialises in aerial photographic work, and has devised a special wing mounted system for film and video cameras. His many awards include a Winston Churchill Fellowship; the Cherry Kearton Medal from the Royal Geographical Society; and film awards include the Genesis Award from the Ark Trust for Conservation; an International Prime Time Emmy; and the Golden Eagle Award from New York.

DAE SASITORN is from Thailand. She came to England to do a postgraduate study in Chemistry many years ago, then had a change of heart to follow her love of nature into the wildlife film making world. She has managed Last Refuge Ltd and its film and photographic archives for the last years. It was not until five years ago that she started doing aerial photography. Under intensive learning of the skill from Adrian, Dae put hundreds of film rolls through the Hasselblad camera and has now become one of the finest aerial photographers. In addition to the photography, Dae undertook the scanning and grading of the images, and also designed this book.

LAST REFUGE Ltd was established in 1992 to document and archive our disappearing natural world through films, images, and research, and to play an educational role in raising public awareness in conservation. The company provides images and film from its growing archives to publishers, broadcasters and interested parties worldwide.

ISBN: 0-9544350-5-2

**All photographs in this book are available as high quality prints
from www.lastrefuge.co.uk**